I0528483

The Spinning Mind of a Volunteer Youth Leader

Sarah Jane Coombs

The Spinning Mind of a Volunteer Youth Leader

Copyright 2023 by Sarah Jane Coombs

All rights reserved

Paperback ISBN 978-1-957497-30-3

Library of Congress Catalog No. XXXXXXX

Published in the United States of America

The Spinning Mind of a Volunteer Youth Leader

Sarah Jane Coombs

To my family who has traveled this journey with me.
Zip, who many times has been the manpower behind
making ministry dreams a reality.
Victoria, Benjamin, Braxton and Levi, who inspired
many of my youth ministry adventures and encouraged
every out of the box idea that was spinning through my
mind. Braxton, I will always hear your voice in my head
saying "You got this mama!"

Endorsements

The Spinning Mind of a Volunteer Youth Leader is a fun look behind the curtain into the world of leading student ministries. Sarah's vulnerability and transparency from her experience will be an encouragement to youth workers in any context. Her openness into her own struggles, doubts and highlights in ministry are deeply relatable. From her initial calling to faithfully serving, to experiencing the challenge of surrendering a student ministry, it is great to walk alongside Sarah's journey through her writing.

Pastor Wayne Giroux, Director of Student Ministries, Western Ontario District, Pentecostal Assemblies of Canada

The Spinning Mind of a Volunteer Youth Leader by Sarah Jane Coombs reveals the investment, sacrifice and dedication needed to develop an effective ministry that will touch young hearts and change lives forever. Part memoir and part handbook, The Spinning Mind of a Volunteer Youth Leader is full of funny and touching moments gleaned from years of experience that will inspire youth leaders everywhere.

Susan Reimer, Author of the Forged in Flames Trilogy, Penelope, Letters in the Woods, and Strawberry Tea

The Spinning Mind of a Volunteer Youth Leader is a book that will inspire anyone from the seasoned ministry leader to those who are just getting started. The author Sarah Coombs shares her incredible passion to serve and be used by God;

not just in extraordinary ways but in the everyday lives of those around her. As someone who has worked with youth and children, the stories that are shared are easy to relate to; it is encouraging to see the difference that one caring, loving person can make. Leaving you with the knowledge that God desires us to step out in faith to where He is leading.

Sarah Burt, Family Ministries Director, Clearview Community Church

Contents

Jumpin' Off The Page, is the story of how an English assign-ment in high school leads to a lifetime adventure in youth ministry. How the word 'youth' jumps off the page and answers the question ,"What do you want to do with your life?." In this chapter God called me into youth ministry. He took me from being a camp counselor to trying to discover what the adult version of a camp counselor might be.

In Getting There, I discovered that the path from high school to full-time youth ministry was anything but straight. I had plans to go to Bible college, graduate with my social work degree and eventually open a home for teenage girls. Plans changed when love, children, and a college rejection letter took me in a different direction. I learned that when you're trusting God, but the path that you are on doesn't lead you straight to where you think he is calling you to, don't worry. He's just taking you for an adventure along the way.

In chapter three I take you through the process of changing from an open door policy to an open heart policy with teens that I work with. Youth ministry becomes more than just a program but a part of our families everyday home life. My family and the students in the youth program start doing life together. I find similarities between the youth ministry and the early church in the book of Acts as they spend time together learning about the Bible, praying and taking care of each other's needs.

Chapter four introduces Runway Ranch, the family farm. It tells the story of how God provided this property for ministry. If you were to wander the back yard or fields at Runway Ranch at any given time, summer or winter, you would be sure to find evidence of a youth project somewhere, from makeshift camp grounds to paintball bushes. I show how Runway Ranch became more than just the family farm but a home away from home for some of the teens in the youth program. This chapter tells the story of Josh as he joins the Runway Ranch family after his father's death.

More Where That Came From, is a chapter about hearing God's voice and being able to do what He asks you to do. I share times in my life when I hear God speak. I share times when I listened to His voice and rose to the challenge and times when I did not. This chapter is a reminder that when God asks you to do something that he does it for a reason. More Where That Came From includes my brother's near death experience and the three am wake up call to pray that saved his life. This chapter compares using the plans and ideas that God whispers in my ear to the gold coins given to the servants in Matthew 25.

In this chapter I explain my dislike for the phrase 'just a volunteer' and I share my belief that our ministries are stronger, more effective, and probably a whole lot more fun because of the dedicated, talented, and sometimes crazy people who show up and make things happen. I explain how being a volunteer as opposed to paid staff had never made a difference. That my commitment to teens and youth programming wasn't affected by whether or not I received a paycheck. Just A Volunteer, explores the idea behind Go Mad (Make a difference) nights and how they gave the teens an opportunity to really live out some of the lessons that they have been learning. This chapter highlights Mathew 25:40 and shares how providing creative volunteer opportunities for the teens led to an ongoing outreach project in our community.

This chapter explains the title of the book. The image of a mini tornado is used to visualize the thoughts spinning in my head at any given time. I explain the endless flow of creative plans moving through my mind and how I thrive in this busy environment. I share stories of God filling my mind with inspiring and fun ideas in the middle of the night and the realization of why this never happens during the day. In this chapter I discover the importance of following Jesus' example and taking a break to spend some one on one quality time with God.

In chapter 8, I use a comical story about my eyeglasses to introduce the idea of staying focused and lessons from my motorcycle training course are a reminder to focus on where you want to go and not on the obstacles that are in your way. In this chapter, stories from youth ministry demonstrate how the things that I focused on, were the very things that would start changing. Chapter 8 talks about how the most important thing to focus on when working with the teens was their relationship with Jesus. I compare not praying or doing Bible lessons at youth events, to having a birthday party for someone and refusing to invite them.

Dangling The Carrot is an emotional chapter about the journey from volunteer youth director to paid youth Pastor. For years I had been told from different pastors that when the church could afford to, that they would like to offer me a paid position. When a small amount of funds became available many years later the board was looking to hire a part time assistant but hadn't considered making the youth director a paid position. I describe my dramatic response that prompts the pastor to tell the board that the church had been dangling a carrot for years. This chapter shared the intense conversations that took place and the behind the scenes process of transitioning from volunteer to paid staff.

In this Chapter I describe my self diagnosed fake confidence syndrome and the process of claiming my title as a youth pastor. I shared details of my struggle as I wrestled with the questions. "Am I good enough? Am I strong enough?" This chapter includes a story of how a personality test resulted in me being named a roaring lion when I felt like a timid kitten on the inside. Chapter eleven also talks about how the Holy Spirit can transform people and equip them for whatever it is that He calls them to do.

In this chapter my yo-yo collection is used to introduce the ups and downs of youth ministry and the idea that God doesn't want us to be on an emotional roller coaster. I explain how working with the teens can be exciting and rewarding but at times can be a very heavy load to carry. The Righteous Right Hand includes a vision from God. In the vision, God is holding the teens on a tray in his hand. That vision transformed my view of youth ministry and reminded me that even as a youth Pastor I did not hold up the youth group, God did.

Chapter 12 They Can Hear You   101

They Can Hear You, deals with the question of whether or not Youth Ministry was having an impact on the teens that I worked with. This chapter shares stories of youth who remember powerful words that influenced their lives. I tell about the secret drawer under my bed where the thank you letters are tucked away. These thank you letters talk about how I had changed people's lives. In this chapter I explain that I had not changed anyone's life, that God did that! Chapter twelve compares youth ministry to planting seeds that only God can grow.

Chapter 13 It's Not About You   108

Chapter 13 is the final chapter for youth ministry at the church in Kapuskasing where I had been leading the students for 17 years and the children for years before that. This story follows my emotional journey of saying goodbye and passing the symbolic torch to the next youth leader. I share the defining moment that God whispered "It's not about you." I share the thought that if you have no idea what you want to do next in your life, then you are in the perfect place for God to call you into something that you may never have thought of on your own. I was in that place.

Chapter 1

Jumpin' Off the Page

"If you have a passion for something, a non-stop desire to accomplish a certain task, a jump off the page word in your life, then consider that God may be leading you into the very thing that you were designed for."

Sarah Jane

Bright stage lights flashed through the wooden beams while giant speakers surrounded by hay bales blasted upbeat worship music. A hundred and twenty students and leaders from across Northern Ontario danced to the beat of the live band playing in the loft of our barn, stirring up dust as they jumped up and down on the dirt floor. I stepped outside the sliding barn door and called in a few more teenagers that were bouncing balls on the old cement pad that we called a basketball court. I had a heart for these teens; a deep passion was growing within me.

When did this all start? I don't really know; maybe in the high school library. I'm not sure which teacher sent us there—probably my English teacher. She was young and had short, bright-red hair, which was ironic since her name was Ms. White. I always found Ms. White to be a little more creative and a little less traditional than the other high school teachers. That's what makes me think that she's the teacher who sent us to the library on this soul-searching assignment. The assignment was to answer a specific question, a question with the potential to excite or exhaust any teenager, any day, anywhere. The question was, "What do you want to do with your life?"

The assignment was to flip through magazines and newspapers looking for job descriptions or career opportunities that we would possibly want to do when we grew up—maybe an ad that got us excited about what might come next when our high school years were over. I remember flipping open a huge newspaper page that took up half the round library table. The page was filled with help wanted and career choices. It definitely wasn't a local paper. I grew up in Northern Ontario, and there was no way all those jobs were available in my hometown. It looked like a big city newspaper to me. I

Jumping off the Page

glanced up and down the columns looking for something that interested me. Nope, nope, nope, uh, uh, nope, nothing. I changed newspapers and looked through magazines, but I wasn't interested in any of those career choices. I may have ripped out a couple of "just in case I don't find anything good" kind of ads to use in my assignment, but nothing jumped off the page at me. Nothing really grabbed my attention and said, "Hey, this is what you want to do with your life."

Then I saw it.

The ad said, "youth counselor services." At the time, I had no idea what that really was, but the word "youth" *did* jump off the page at me as if it was printed in bold, italics, underlined, and perhaps even flashing in neon. The word "youth" stirred up something inside of me and still does to this day. As I said, I had no idea what youth counseling service was, but I knew what I wanted it to be.

When I was a kid, my favorite place, other than home, was Newport, a summer camp in the Muskoka area. It was a three-hour trip to get there, but I was there every chance I could get, from summer camps to youth events, winter retreats to leadership training. If there was camp, I was there. At 14, I took my counselor-in-training course. We called it C.I.T for short. Being a C.I.T was a moment of transition—too cool to still be a camper but not cool enough to be called staff. I passed my C.I.T. course, signed on as staff, and took up residence at the camp every summer until I got married; literally, I had my wedding there.

Every summer, I had the same job: girls' counselor. I counseled both junior and senior girls, but senior girls were my favorite. It was less like babysitting and more like having a significant impact on someone's life.

I knew that youth counselor services couldn't possibly mean being a camp counselor as a full-time career, but this was the job post that jumped off the page, so this is the job post

I ripped out and glued into my assignment. Did Ms. White enjoy my presentation? Did she give me a good grade? I have no idea. I'm less impressed with the impact the assignment had on my grades than the significant impact it had on my life. It was a defining moment. A jump-off-the-page realization. I wanted to work with youth. Youth, teenagers, high school students, whatever you call them—these are the young people that I realized had and still have a special place in my heart.

On paper, the "what you want to do with your life" assignment was done and handed in, but in reality, it was just beginning. New task, answer this: what *was* the grown-up version of a camp counselor?

One of the lessons I teach over and over again to the young people I work with is that they were created with a purpose and that God has given them different gifts and talents that make them uniquely designed for a reason. If you have a passion for something, a non-stop desire to accomplish a certain task, a jump-off-the-page word in your life, then consider that God may be leading you into the very thing that you were designed for. There in the high school library, at the age of 15 or 16, I realized that working with teenagers was the direction God was leading me. A passion for student ministry started growing within me.

There was an after-school ministry for kids on Tuesday nights at my church, and I began teaching. I liked it; it was a creative outlet for me. I was a part of that program when I was a kid, so I already knew the stories and lessons. As a teacher, I liked to put a creative spin on things. I would show up early and rearrange the room to fit whatever theme

I found in the lesson. I had access to an entire wall of cupboards and a storage room full of costumes, decorations, and building materials. I even switched out the furniture sometimes. The kids never knew what they were going to walk into. One day the story had to do with people traveling from town to town and setting up tents. I piled chairs like a pyramid on top of tables and covered them with old stage curtains to build a massive tent in the middle of the church basement. It's beyond me why an adult didn't step in, tell me how crazy I was, and how I had created a giant danger zone that the kids really shouldn't be allowed to enter, but no one did. So, we sat under tables eating our snacks and learning about travelers wandering in the desert for 40 years.

At the same time, my friend Dianna and I took over leadership of our youth group. We were the perfect team. I'd always been a back-of-the-classroom, quiet kind of kid, and Dianna was the opposite. She was outgoing, talked to anyone, and had no problem gathering everyone's attention and making things happen. It was a good system. I would come up with creative ideas, work out all the behind-the-scenes stuff, and Dianna would take it from there. There was a pastor who did the preaching and teaching, but we took care of the rest. We were good friends, and we made a great team.

Every year the camp hosted a ski weekend. One year, Dianna and I decided that instead of just taking the church van with our regular group of teens, we would promote this thing like crazy, invite everyone and anyone, and see if we could fill a bus. We did. A bus and a pick-up truck, to be more specific. God had placed a jump-off-the-page desire in my heart and given me a partner who shared my passion and plenty of opportunities to work with other students my age.

One day, the school librarian, who I believe also did some work with the school guidance office, approached me about a new program they were creating. The school was starting up a youth hotline. The training was done after school hours but counted as a half credit on our report cards. The training wasn't intense, but it was enough to make us feel confident when we answered the calls. I had to keep reminding myself that it wasn't my job to tell the caller what to do, but it was my job to listen and help them come up with their own best possible solution to their problem.

I remember one student whose friend had run away from home. They called in because they were torn about whether or not to tell their friend's mom. I asked her, "What might happen if you don't tell her mom?" The caller thought that through. Then I asked, "What might happen if you do tell her mom?" The caller thought *that* through. Then I asked, "What do you think you should do?" She quickly responded with, "Hang on, I'll call you right back; I have to go call my friend's mom" That's the only specific conversation that I remember.

Most of my calls were from other teens who were lonely and just wanted to talk. Some calls were from teens who were angry and needed to vent. They had no idea who they were talking to. It's the one time in my life that I had a secret identity. My name was Lisa. We were told in our training that we needed a fake name to protect our identity at school and help prevent conversations from becoming personal. We didn't need a back story because we weren't supposed to talk about ourselves. We just needed a name. I don't know why I chose that name; there really was no special reason. When I was a kid and played make-believe with my friends, I would call myself Bonnie. Bonnie was my older cousin, and, as a kid, she was the prettiest girl I knew. If I wanted to be anyone, I wanted to be Bonnie. I suppose by the time I reached high school, I was good with being me. I was no longer a 'Bonnie wannabe.' I was now Lisa, the youth hotline worker.

The same librarian who offered me a position on the youth hotline also asked me if I would connect with a student who had just moved to Canada from Hong Kong. I'm sure she had a fancy name for it—student liaison, peer sponsor, or something like that, but when you get right down to it, she was just asking me to be his friend. His name was Jason, but Jason wasn't his real name. No one could pronounce his real name, so they changed his name to Jason when he came to Canada. The year before, when the word "youth" had jumped off the page at me, it was clearly in English. I wouldn't have expected that one of my first youth projects would involve working with someone who couldn't speak the language. Jason was actually a university student but had to spend a year in high school English class before he could go on to his university program. We could barely communicate; we talked with our hands, pointed, and even scribbled drawings on paper just so we could understand each other.

I taught Jason that when you meet someone in Canada, you shake hands instead of bowing. I forgot to tell him that it only happens the first time you meet or if you haven't seen someone in a while. *Oops, my bad.* I realized we needed to

revisit that lesson when I saw him walking down the hallway at school, shaking hands with everyone who made
eye contact with him. Our inability to communicate could
have been frustrating, but it wasn't; it was fun introducing
someone to a totally different way of life.

We were walking along the sidewalk one day when Jason
began repeating himself. He just kept saying, "What is it?
What is it?" When he pointed to the sky, I realized that
while I was experiencing the first snowfall of the year, Jason was experiencing the first snowfall of his life.

Was this it? Was this the grown-up version of a camp counselor: being a peer sponsor, teaching after-school programs
to kids, planning youth events, working on the hotline?
Could this be the reason that the word "youth" jumped off
the page in the school library? Was this the plan and the
purpose which God had designed for me?

> *"For we are God's handiwork, created in Christ Jesus to do good*
> *works, which God prepared in advance for us to do."*
>
> *Ephesians 2:10 NIV*

Chapter 2

Getting There

"When you're trusting God but the path that you are on doesn't lead you straight to where you think he is calling you to, don't worry. He's just taking you for an adventure along the way."

~Sarah Jane

Everyone was taking their turn, and now it was mine. In alphabetical order, all of the grade 12 students were called to the guidance office. When I walked in, the table was covered with course catalogs for all of the colleges in Ontario. The guidance counselor was ready with her clipboard. She was going to talk me through then help me decide the "furthering your education" process. That wasn't necessary; I already knew exactly what I wanted to do.

At the time, students who planned to attend university needed to take the five-year program. I had one more year to make college choices, but I didn't need the year. I had a plan. I was going to Bible college. I was going to graduate with my social work degree and eventually open a home for teenage girls. That was the plan. I guess the guidance counselor was happy with that because she didn't try to talk me out of it. She did have a ton of questions for me, though, all about the Bible college. What was the name? Where was it located? How did I know about it? She apologized for asking so many questions but said she was extremely interested. She went on to say that I wasn't the first student to mention it and that she had already seen the name of the Bible college on people's lists of the top five places they might like to attend. I was just as surprised as she was. This was our church Bible college. I was pretty sure that the only place that local teens would have heard about it was at our youth group. I was impressed. I knew that Dianna and I were bringing a lot of students in and that several of them were becoming serious about church and Jesus. Were they also considering Bible college? That was cool. As I was about to leave the room, the guidance counselor asked me if I would bring her a copy of the Bible college catalog so that she could add it to her pile of available options.

I didn't need to go back for a second meeting in the guidance office. I had everything figured out, or so I thought. Two summers before high school graduation, I met Zip. His real name is Tim, but everyone I knew called him Zip. The first time I saw Tim was at a seminar that we both attended. He was sitting beside me when we were asked to fill out a form. The form had a checkbox option of married or single. Tim added a checkbox and wrote "available" beside it. He put a checkmark in the "available" box and slid it over for me to see. That was just a tiny taste of what a big flirt this guy was. We started dating that summer. I was still living at home in Northern Ontario, and Tim was living 6 hours away, but we had both been hired as summer staff at Camp Newport.

Newport had always been an important place for me, and it held special memories for Tim as well. With the open field, the chapel in the pines, and sunsets over the beach, it was the perfect place for a wedding. Tim and I were married there the summer I graduated high school.

Tim had been offered a job as a ramp attendant at the London airport, and we were headed off to the city. If you had asked me a year before, I would not have thought that London, Ontario was the city I would be living in. The Bible college was in Winnipeg, Manitoba. There were 2000 km between where I was and where I thought I would be. I had a plan, and I thought it was a good one. A year and a half earlier, before I met with the counselor in the school guidance office, I had marked out a path of where I felt God was leading me and how I thought I would get there. The path I was on seemed to be taking me in an entirely different direction. I had no regrets. I was married to the man I loved, and every day was a new adventure.

I still felt led to work with teenagers, but I was no longer dreaming of opening a girl's home. Perhaps it was the jealous insecurities of a teenage bride, or wisdom beyond my years, but a new husband and a house full of teenage girls didn't seem like a good idea. I still wanted to do youth ministry, but I wasn't sure how that was going to happen.

Our apartment was only blocks away from Fanshawe College. There were two months until fall classes started. It was last minute, but I thought maybe if I applied right away, I might get accepted for school in the fall. I applied for their child and youth worker program. I was hoping to get started working with youth, but all I got was a rejection letter. The child and youth worker program was full. They offered me a position in the early childhood education program, but

I wasn't interested.

I knew that I had been called to youth ministry of some kind, but I had no idea how I was going to get there. I no longer had a plan or a path marked out to take me where I thought that I should be, but I was trusting God. I knew that the Bible said to "trust in the Lord with all your heart and lean not on your own understanding, in all your ways submit to Him and he will make your paths straight." Proverbs 3:5,6 NIV

I had only been going to the church in London for a couple of months when the children's director told me that she was stepping down. She asked if I would volunteer to lead the children's ministry. I was thankful for the opportunity and started right away. It was only a Sunday morning program. There was a large group of kids, but it didn't require a lot of time or energy to make it happen. It was less than part-time hours. Tim was busy at work during the day, and when I wasn't at the church, I was bored. One day I told him, "I either need to get a job or start a family." I think God heard us, chuckled, and said, "How about both?" I got a job at a donut factory around the same time that I became pregnant with Victoria. It was a large factory with conveyor belts full of donuts that got delivered around town.

My job was to fry the donuts in a giant fryer, put them on the conveyor, and catch them at the end before they fell off. Every day, my baby belly was getting bigger and bigger. One day, the boss told me that he was taking me off the fryer and putting me on decorating. I asked him why, and he pointed at my apron. There was a straight yellow oil line across my belly where the hot tray of donuts was resting while I carried them from the fryer to the conveyor. I hadn't even noticed.

When Victoria was born, I went on maternity leave from the donut factory but kept doing children's ministry. We only lived a block away from the church, so I would walk over before the church service to do the children's program, and Tim would get Victoria ready for church (My friends and I would joke about being able to tell who got her ready by what she looked like when she got there). I continued to do children's ministry but really had a passion for teens. When the junior/senior high teacher stepped down, I stepped in. You could tell by the amount of energy that went into the teen class versus the children's ministry, but that was where my heart was. We had the class over for barbeques and did activities at the church outside of Sunday morning classes.

We had been living in London for just over two years when Tim's dad passed away. We got the call in the middle of the night, and Tim left the next morning to be with his mom. Over the next couple of months, Tim spent a lot of time traveling back and forth from London to Lindsay, where his mom lived. I felt a move coming on, and I was right. It wasn't long before Tim, Victoria, and I moved to Lindsay, Ontario, to live with my mother-in-law. Tim and his brother Dan took over his father's trucking business and spent most of their time on the road.

I wasn't happy; I missed being together as a family. My sister-in-law said I needed to stop spending all my time waiting for Tim to come home and just start doing things that I liked to do. I didn't want to. This is the one time in my life that I was angry with God and didn't mind telling him that.

I was lying in my bed one night, thinking about how unhappy I was. I began to pray. I was giving God a piece of my mind. I know; I should have been praying for patience or wisdom or something like that. The right thing to do probably would have been to pray for direction and guidance, but I didn't. He gave it to me anyway. I felt an overwhelming sense of urgency inside of me. I leaned off the side of my bed as far as I could without losing my balance and falling on my head. I was reaching for a box of things that were still packed from our move to Lindsay several months before. I slid my hand into the box and pulled out an old Bible college catalog that I had been holding onto since high school. My heart was racing as I held the course catalog in my hand. I knew it was time. This was really going to happen.

After the donut factory in London, I would've been happy if I had never seen another donut again, but when we moved to Lindsay, I took a job at a donut shop. I had money saved that I could use for school. Tim's mom said that I could keep my summer rent money and put it towards tuition. With the money I had saved, plus a student loan and some help from Tim, going away to school really was a possibility. Tim said that instead of making his stops in Lindsay, he could make them in Winnipeg so that he could spend time with Victoria and me.

I applied for the social work program. I was sending a last-minute college application again, but this time I got accepted. We loaded my car on the back of the transport trailer and headed west. When we left for Winnipeg, I had no apartment and no childcare. We had no choice but to trust that if this was where God was leading us, then He would work out the details. God was *definitely* working out the details. When we arrived at the college, we were greeted by an old camp friend, and she held out a key. She had secured for us an apartment in her building. The building was across the street and a few blocks down from the college. It was a three-story walk-up, and our apartment would be on the top floor. They called it the White House, not only because it was painted white but because, for years, it had been home to different student body presidents.

The next day we registered Victoria for daycare. The lady who was filling out our paperwork asked us for our address. We asked if she wanted my address in Winnipeg or Tim's address back home. She looked surprised and said, "You guys don't live together? You're a single mom?" I explained that I was not a single mom, that we were happily married, and that Tim was still taking care of us financially. He just wasn't able to move to Winnipeg. She ripped up the paperwork that she had been filling out. She said it didn't matter how happily married we were, that if we had separate addresses, I qualified as a single mom, and our daycare expenses would be covered. We only needed to pay the eighteen dollars a month administration fee.

The daycare was an easy walk from the apartment. It was around the corner at the University of Winnipeg. I wasn't going to need the car and didn't want the large parking fees. Tim loaded the car on the trailer and took it back to Ontario. Then he headed out on the road. It was time for Victoria and me to start our Bible college adventure.

A couple of months into the first semester, one of our classes went on a field trip. It was a Sunday morning, and we were doing a service at a very unique church downtown. Anyone could attend this church, but it was specifically designed as an outreach for people who were living rough lives in the downtown area. These were some of the people that we could be working with when we graduated with our social work degree. The church gave out meal tickets during the service for anyone who wanted to stay for a free lunch. This church attracted hundreds of people who were living on the streets. The church began to fill up with prostitutes and drug addicts. This church was amazing. It was meeting people's needs both spiritually and physically. I was glad I got to be a part of the service, but I realized that it was a terrible idea to have brought my two-year-old daughter into this environment. We were sitting near the front with other Bible college students. When I got up to do my part on the platform, someone took my seat right beside Victoria. I could tell from his body language that he was probably drunk. I had a terrible feeling in the pit of my stomach, so as soon as I finished my part, I stepped off the platform and sat on Victoria's chair with her on my lap. I decided that day that I did not want to pursue social work. I knew myself. I knew that when I took something on that I was all in, and this wasn't something that I wanted Victoria to be involved with.

I had my mind so set on the social work program that I hadn't explored other options. I wanted to work with teenagers. I thought that social work was the way to go, but the college offered a youth pastor program. Although I hadn't looked into it before, I realized it should've been my first choice all along. It was easy to switch over, as the first-year courses were the same. Every student would graduate with a biblical certificate. I felt like God had taken me on several detours but that I was now on the straight path to youth ministry. I was wrong.

After the first semester, I started experiencing morning sickness. The doctor at the drop-in clinic gave me a stern lecture about teen pregnancy and being a single mom. I didn't bother telling him that I wasn't a teenager, I wasn't single, and this wasn't my first pregnancy. It was just too much fun watching him make a fool of himself. Regardless of his terrible bedside manner, he was able to confirm that there was a baby growing inside of me.

Despite the fact that I used to throw up during morning classes and fall asleep in afternoon classes, I still managed to graduate with honors. I graduated with my biblical certificate but wasn't going back in September. I had debated returning to classes and having both Victoria and baby Benjamin in daycare, but he would have only been one month old when school started in September, and there was no way I was going to do that. I was happy to go back home to Lindsay.

Tim had been offered a job as a flight instructor at Lindsay Airport. He and his brother had decided to sell the truck and work close to home where they could spend time with their families. Tim's aviation plans were back on track; my youth ministry ones, not so much. It wasn't long before I was offered a volunteer position at the church in Lindsay. The person who had been running the children's ministry was transitioning into being a foster care parent, and the church was looking for someone to run the children's program. I accepted the position, and I loved it. It was more than just running a Sunday School program. I was able to start a midweek program and family activities. It was a lot of work, but it was worth it. When the teen class teacher moved away, I started teaching the teens as well. I had also created a junior high program that was attracting so many neighborhood kids, I had to ask the pastor to find me some help. I really felt like God was using me to make a difference.

I soon discovered that the twists and turns in my path to youth ministry weren't over yet. Tim had applied for a flying job in Kapuskasing, Ontario. I remembered the name from our trip to Winnipeg years before, but I never would have guessed that one day we would be living that far north. Tim was hired as a pilot for Commercial Aviation and started right away. It was only a few months until Victoria finished her grade 1 school year, so Victoria, Benjamin, and I stayed behind. I took that time to plan and organize at the church and to get the programs ready to pass on to someone else. Tim came back and forth to Lindsay to visit and to move our things one truckload at a time.

By the end of the school year, most of our things had already been taken to our new home. When the kids and I finally joined Tim, he had the apartment all setup. He had put together the bunk beds using the same sheets and blankets that the kids always used. Their books and their toys were on the same shelves in their cabinets, and their favorite stuffed animals were on their pillows, waiting for them. Tim certainly knew how to make the transition easier.

Youth ministry didn't look very promising in our new church. There was no youth programming, and there were only four kids the first Sunday we attended: Victoria, Benjamin, and the pastor's two children. The pastor's wife said that it was a summer thing, that families with kids would disappear every summer. I guess when you live in snow-covered Kapuskasing, you take advantage of the warm weather when it comes around. Families were on vacation or at cottages and campgrounds every weekend. The pastor's wife ran the children's program for our four kids all summer long. She was right; come September, the church started filling up again, and Sunday school teachers went back on the schedule.

Not long after that, we learned our pastors would be leaving. They asked if I would be willing to take over the children's ministry. I really did believe that God was leading me into youth ministry, but every path we took seemed to lead us to the doorstep of a church that needed someone to run their children's program. I said yes, and that was the start of an amazing 22 years of ministry in Kapuskasing. I took nearly a year off when my son Braxton was born and a couple of months off when Levi came along, but my heart was in ministry, and I didn't want to stop. I was exactly where I wanted to be, and it was worth the detours. When I think about the Bible verse that says when you trust in the Lord that he will make your paths straight, I have to shake my head and smirk a little because my path to youth ministry was anything but straight. I realize the verse is really talking about guiding and directing your path, and *that* he certainly did.

What began with a children's program grew into something even more powerful. An entire ministry for children, families, junior high, and youth. Yes, youth. I learned that when you're trusting God, but the path that you are on doesn't lead you straight to where you think he is calling you to, don't worry. He's just taking you on an adventure along the way. My passion for young people and my desire to make a difference in their lives was no longer a possibility. It was a reality.

Trust in the Lord with all your heart and lean not on your own understanding; in all your ways submit to him, and he will make your paths straight. Proverbs 3:5-6 NIV

Chapter 3

Open Heart Policy

"It wasn't until I started volunteering with teens again that God helped us to transform our open door policy into an open heart policy, and the teens I worked with became a part of our family."
~Sarah Jane

As a youth leader, I liked to plan games; group games, individual games, messy games, mystery games, and cool games that the teens can have fun with. I understand the importance of games, how they break down inhibitions, allow kids to work together toward a common goal, and create a relaxed atmosphere. If you hit the right games, you may even have your youth rolling on the floor in a fit of laughter. Games are good. In youth ministry, you need games. I'm not saying that you *can't* do youth ministry without games, but I am saying that you probably shouldn't.

As much as I like to plan games, I really don't like playing them. I never have, even when I was a teen. Card games, yes; board games, sure, but those upfront drink soda through a sock kinda games, no, thank you! I was looking at an old photo album the other day and I saw a picture from my days at camp. It was a picture of a row of teenagers singing an action song, one of those crazy silly songs where you'd have to do ridiculous actions. I remember the song. It was "Singing in the Rain." We'd sing the verse over and over again, but with each verse, we would add a new action, like arms up, butt out, knees together, and turn around. We'd pretty much look deformed by the end of the song. In the picture, everyone was striking a crazy pose, everyone except me. I was standing perfectly normal with my arms crossed and a "what's the matter with these people?" look on my face. Don't get me wrong. I was having a good time. I love watching people do silly songs and play crazy games. I just don't like playing them myself. Even as an adult, when I'm in a group of people and I hear the words, "We're going to play a game," I want to sink down into my chair.

This is the feeling I got the night of the toilet paper game.

I didn't go out much, but two of the ladies from my church were starting up a woman's group. They invited several ladies to an evening out at one of their homes, and I decided to go. We filled our plates with lots of fancy desserts that were displayed in the kitchen and chatted with other ladies as they came in. The hostess asked us to gather in the living room, and it wasn't long before someone said, "We're going to play a game." I may have had a smile on my face, but on the inside, I remembered how much I do not like playing games. The hostess brought out a roll of toilet paper. What were we going to play? I was sure they weren't going to make us wrap each other up like Halloween mummies; cool game, but maybe not for this crowd. They passed the toilet paper around and told us to break off as many squares as we wanted. I had no idea what the game was, nor did I know how many squares I should take in order to get out of the game the fastest. I broke off two toilet paper squares.

"Ok, everyone," the hostess said, "we'll start over here and go around the circle. For every square of toilet paper you broke off, you have to tell us something about yourself that not everyone knows."

Oh, that was it? Say something about myself? No silly faces, no holding random people's hands and seeing if we can untangle ourselves, no weird version of toilet paper twister? Just say something about ourselves. That's not a game; that's an icebreaker, different story. I could do that.

As the ladies began sharing about themselves, the atmosphere in the room began to change. They weren't just saying, "Hey, this is my name, this is where I work, I like to bake cookies and knit mittens." No, they were sharing some deep stuff. Every toilet paper square represented an adventure, a challenge, or a heartbreak. "Hi, my name is Sarah Jane, and I love Reese's peanut butter cups" wasn't going to cut it. I needed to say something deeper, something that was important to me, something I was passionate about. This is what I said: " My name is Sarah, and I have two families." Well, that definitely got everyone's attention. Most of them already knew my name, so it must have been the "I have two families" part that made heads turn so quickly.

I explained. "My first family is my husband Tim and our children, Victoria, Benjamin, Braxton, and Levi. My second family is the students that I volunteer with at the church." I didn't say I had two families because I was craving attention or being dramatic. I wanted to share that I was a volunteer youth leader, but just saying that didn't capture what a huge part of my life youth ministry really was. Actually, I shouldn't have said two families because that's not really true. It's always been one family, one big family, my husband, our children, and youth ministry.

Not long after Tim and I were married, we started a college and careers group. We lived in a small two-bedroom apartment on the seventh floor. Every Monday night, we would open the doors to young adults. Tim would prepare a lesson. I would make sure the apartment was clean, the cookies were baked, and a jug of lemonade was ready. Since then, we have had many different homes, yet the doors have remained open. From that college and careers group on the seventh floor to the young adults' group in our loft at London airport, from a study group in the kitchen of my college rental in Winnipeg to Bible studies in my mother-in-law's unfinished basement, we've always welcomed people with open doors.

From the time our children were born, child and youth programming has been a part of their lives. When I went away to college, Victoria was three. She was my sidekick. While Tim was trucking, the open road had become home for him and his brother. I was experiencing a tiny bit of what it was like to be a single mom. We had arranged daycare while I was in morning and afternoon classes, but for any evening and weekend activities, I'd show up with a little girl on my hip.

One of those activities was a leadership assignment. Everyone was given different public speaking and leadership activities. Because I had Victoria with me, my assignment was to lead a song during the Good Friday service at one of the local churches. They asked me to take Victoria on stage with me and lead a version of *Jesus Loves the Little Children* before the kids were dismissed for their classes. Probably the easiest assignment ever given out in that class. Victoria and I stood hand-in-hand on the stage. I told everyone what number the song was and waited a moment for pages to flip. I said, "Let's sing together," and waited a moment for the music to start. Then I did it. I dramatically pretended to sing every word of that song without any actual sound coming out of my mouth. They didn't need me to lead them. It was a hundred-year-old church song that everyone already knew. I was actually doing them a favor by pretending to sing into the mic. Like I said before, God has gifted us all with different talents and abilities. Singing is definitely not my gift. I got a passing grade and applause after the song. I assume the applause was for the angelic-looking blond-haired girl holding my hand and, in her sweet little voice, actually singing *Jesus Loves the Little Children*. Thanks, kid.

As a children's ministry leader, some years later, the church nursery became my office. I would drop Victoria off at school, and baby Benjamin and I would set up shop in the most practical room available—the one with the toys, the high chair, and the crib. Working from home wasn't a thing back then, nor was online kids programming or digital design for children's ministry. The change table became my desktop. Yes, I know; looking back, that doesn't really seem like a very sanitary decision. But that's what it was: a changing table covered with clip art books, scissors, glue sticks, blank white paper, tape, and colored Crayola markers. This room had everything you needed to create a great poster in a non-digital world and keep a baby happy at the same time.

As the kids got older and the family got bigger, we were all a part of youth ministry. Our open-door policy remained the same, only now there were a lot more play dates.

By this time, we had moved to Kapuskasing. While Tim flew the skies over Northern Ontario, I began to volunteer, first with children and then with youth. It wasn't until I started volunteering with teens again that God helped us to transform our open-door policy into an open-heart policy, and the teens I worked with became a part of our family.

I do understand the importance of boundaries. If you work with students, you've probably been taught to keep a certain amount of distance between your personal life and theirs. I don't have a problem with that, not exactly. Rules are rules for a reason. I've just never been very good at following those particular rules. So many of the youth that I've volunteered with over the years were more than just students in a youth ministry; they were family, even if only for a short time.

I was recently asked to guest-speak at our home church. They were in the middle of a series about teamwork, and I was asked to preach from the book of Acts, a message on the early church and what made them such a great team. As I prepared the message, I was reminded how followers of Jesus had learned about God together, prayed together, hung out with each other all the time, took care of each other, and ate meals together in their homes. Basically, they lived life together as one big family. This is an excellent example for youth ministry today. Digging into the Bible together, praying together, hanging out, taking care of each other, not just within the walls of a church but really living life together.

We had started living life together with our students. It was never a conscious decision; it just happened. We loved the students and didn't mind sharing our lives with them.

Tim was a soccer guy; he played for the Kapuskasing Longhorns, and they had games after church during the summer. Tim would sneak off right after the last song and change into his soccer uniform in the front seat of his pickup truck in order to make it to his game on time. I would load up the minivan, pick up a couple of family meals at the grocery store and head over to the soccer field for the afternoon. There was an open invitation for any teens who wanted to join us. They always did. I don't know if it was the thrill of the game or the smell of chicken tenders and potato wedges, but youth always showed up. Chances are it wasn't the game or the family meal deal that kept them coming, but the opportunity to hang out together as one big family.

These weren't the only soccer games that brought us together like a family. All four of our kids played on soccer teams, all four, and sometimes at the same time on different fields. Tim's job took him out of town a lot, so I was the only parent on soccer duty. I wasn't alone, though. Every Tuesday and Thursday, a group of girls from the youth group would join in our soccer night and watch the games with me. When I had to miss a game because the boys played on different fields, the girls would cover for me. I was extremely thankful for these mini-soccer moms. When the boys were older and didn't need me on the sidelines, I'd walk the track that ran around the soccer field. Guess who walked with me? That's right, mini soccer moms. They were there for me when I needed them, and I was there when they needed me. We were living life together.

One Sunday afternoon, we invited the youth to come to the farm and do hay with us. When people think of doing chores on the farm, unless they've lived the farm life, they tend to get confused between fantasy and reality. They picture radiant sunbeams streaming through the open loft doors while young people in jean overalls and cowboy boots move fluffy piles of wheat with a pitchfork from one end of the loft to the other. Children swing on ropes and land on piles of loose hay, and the farmer squirts milk at the kittens while milking the cows. That's the *fantasy*.

We invited the youth to help bring in the hay. The bales are heavy, the hay scratches, the loft is uncomfortably hot on sunny days, the hay elevator is extremely noisy, and the air is thick with hay dust. That is the reality. We told them it would be hard work and that the only payment would be unlimited glasses of lemonade. I expected a couple of students to rise to the challenge, but what I didn't expect was that there would be 17 people working in the hay that day, including one teenage girl with a broken leg. We even had some parents join in. The parents reminisced about working on a farm as kids and talked about how it's good for the teens to experience some old-fashioned hard work. The students who showed up that day weren't there for the hard work. They didn't come for the lemonade or to jump from a swinging rope onto a pile of hay (we actually did have that part of the fantasy). They were there because they were part of a family. We had become a group of people who relied on each other and helped each other out. We were living life together.

What had started as an open-door policy had changed over the years. It wasn't just ministries and programs that were a part of our family life but the students themselves. They became a part of our everyday lives. Just like the church in the book of Acts, we were one big family living life together.

> *And all the believers met together constantly and shared every-thing with each other.*
>
> *Acts 2:44*

Chapter 4

Runway Ranch

"Runway Ranch was more than just our home, it was a part of youth ministry, and I wouldn't have had it any other way."

~Sarah Jane

It was cold, and the back road I was driving down was covered with snow. Probably wasn't the best day to head out for a drive, but while the older kids were at school and Tim was at work, I packed up Levi, our youngest boy, in our blue Pontiac Montana and headed out. It was a twelve-minute drive from Kapuskasing and only a six-minute drive from the airport.

When our family moved to Kapuskasing five years earlier, we had wanted to find a place in the country, but it didn't happen. We had only planned on being in Kap for a couple of months while Tim did his training, so we rented a small two-bedroom apartment. It was tiny, really tiny. If I wanted to do a tour of the apartment, I could stand in the living room pointing in any direction to give the grand tour: bathroom, bedroom, bedroom, kitchen, and done. We stayed there for close to two years. Benjamin and Victoria shared a room, and when Braxton was born, he slept in a bassinet beside our bed. There wasn't enough room for a crib. When

I was pregnant with Levi, we decided that a family of six in that tiny apartment might drive us crazy. It was time to look for a house, so that's what we did, and for the past three years, we had been living on Spruce St. in Kapuskasing.

I really liked our house on Spruce Street. It was an average home, nothing elaborate, but it was pretty. The floors were hardwood, some of the doorways had arches, and there was a large back entrance with skylights. I'm sure my husband would describe it in a much more masculine way, but to me, it was pretty. We had created a lot of memories, and I didn't really like the idea of leaving, but we had always wanted a place in the country, and the timing was right.

There were some great kids on Spruce Street, and our yard was always full of extra children. Unfortunately, there were also some troublemakers. Cursing and swearing, vandalizing property, and pushing the other kids around was just a typical day for some of the boys. I knew that it was our responsibility to love these boys, to be compassionate and kind to them, which we were, but I also knew it was our responsibility to protect our children from negative influences and potentially harmful situations. These boys were just a little older than Benjamin, so naturally, they wanted to spend time together. I don't know if you've ever experienced that gut feeling that something will end badly, but that's the feeling I would get when Ben went out to play. I wasn't the kind of mom that worried about every move my children would make, but this was different. This gut feeling, perhaps a mother's instinct or a nudge from the Holy Spirit, was a warning for us. It was a good time to find that place in the country that we had always wanted. I later learned that by the time Benjamin had finished high school, all three of the Spruce Street boys had seen the inside of a prison cell.

The day I drove out to the farm is a day I will always remember. I pulled over on the side of the road in front of a white and green, fairly modest-looking home with a *for sale* sign in the window. I would have pulled into the driveway, but no one was living there at the time, and the driveway wasn't plowed. There were two houses on the property, the main house, white with green shutters, and a smaller kind of beat-up-looking house with worn-out, blue-painted siding. There was a huge barn in the backyard, one section made of original barn board and a large addition made from lumber and tin. The farm had a grass strip runway in the field beside the house. We had been told it was there but hadn't seen it since the fields were covered with snow. We'd already put in an offer to buy the farm. A little crazy, considering that I had never seen the inside of the houses or the barn. Tim had been through the house on a back concession road near the village of Val Rita with a real estate agent maybe a week before, but I stayed home with the kids. The offer we put in on the house wasn't likely to be accepted. We offered half of the asking price. Half! Who does that? Tim does. He's a bargain hunter and never pays full price for anything if he can help it.

When we bought the house on Spruce Street, we discovered that the seller was a sales rep for Schneider Meats. We closed the deal for less than the asking price, plus a case of bacon. The lawyers agreed with the arrangement but refused to put the meat deal in the contract. Not only did we get the house and the case of bacon, but we got a case of bologna as well.

This time we offered half the asking price. We had decided that if they came back with a counteroffer, even though that was a normal thing to do, we would look somewhere else.

I hadn't planned to drive to the farm that day, but I felt drawn to it. I sat in the van on the side of the road, and I prayed. I'm pretty sure these are the exact words I prayed: "Dear God, if you give us this house, I'll use it for you." Was I in the habit of trying to strike a deal with God? Did I think I had some kind of leverage with the all-knowing, all-powerful creator of the universe? No, but that's what I said to Him. "If you give us this house, I'll use it for you."

I meant what I said. I could already picture it. A yard full of teenagers, bonfires, campouts, field games, Bible studies; so much potential. God *did* give us the farm with no counteroffer. That summer, we named our property and painted the name Runway Ranch in big, bold green letters across the front of the barn.

I truly believe that what I thought was making a deal with God was really just agreeing to something that God had already planned out for us long before we saw a *for sale* sign in the window. I once heard a woman say that the best way to get her husband to do something she wanted was to let him think that it was his idea in the first place. I may or may not have tried this on my own husband from time to time. Perhaps God was using this technique on me. Providing us with the perfect location for youth ministry, a potential home away from home for some of our students, and then allowing me to think that I came up with this idea on my own.

When we first moved to the farm, I was only doing youth activities twice a month. I was pretty busy with our kids, so planning activities on our own property where I could organize and set up without heading into town just made sense. Once a month, the teens would meet at Runway Ranch, and once a month, they would head out of town for youth rallies sponsored by other youth groups throughout the north.

The teens started bringing friends, and their friends started bringing friends, and what had started as two teenage girls and a couple of people they invited had now grown to a group of 15 or more.

The pastor asked if I would consider making it a weekly thing. I was up for the challenge, so I agreed. I agreed to double the amount of time I volunteered, and he agreed to do the lesson once a month and play drums so we could start a youth band. Win-win for me, so I filled the youth calendar with activities for every Friday night. Doing youth ministry every Friday left plenty of opportunity to hold up my end of the deal I had made with God. Runway Ranch was more than just our home; it was a part of youth ministry, and I wouldn't have had it any other way. It didn't take long before I concluded that it was definitely God's idea, His plan. The Bible says that God is able to do immensely more than we could ever ask or even imagine. I never would have imagined such a powerful youth ministry would take place at Runway Ranch.

For the first few years on the farm, when Zip was still working in the north and had more time on his hands, he would be all in when I asked him to take on some pretty crazy youth projects. Random stuff like a hay maze, a riding bull made from a barrel and some ropes, or a pumpkin launcher. He even built a low ropes course in our backyard. He had been trained as an instructor for both high and low ropes courses when he worked at the camp where we first met, so he knew what he was doing. I used the ropes course for team-building exercises and lessons on teamwork. I talked about how God tells us to build each other up and help each other out.

If you wandered the backyard or fields at Runway Ranch at any given time, summer or winter, you would surely find evidence of a youth project somewhere. A makeshift campground, a path from snowshoes, a bush camp, a skidoo trail, a paintball bush, or a plastic Easter egg still hiding in the field when the snow finally melted at the end of April.

The barn at Runway Ranch was the location for many Northern Ontario Youth Rallies. One rally hosted over 100 young people scattered throughout the barn in a giant indoor hay maze. After escaping the maze, they watched the Cities Under Fire tour band play a concert from the loft. The barn concert is featured several times in the Cities Under Fire - Stay official music video on YouTube[1].

The open-heart, open-door policy that we had tried to maintain over the years didn't only extend to the barn and the fields but to our home at Runway Ranch as well.

There is a futon in our rec room. The rec room isn't large. It's big enough for our pool table but not big enough so that the ends of the pool cues don't hit the wall when you're trying to take a shot. In the corner of the room is the futon; it's an old, beat-up, falling apart futon. We all agree that it's time for the futon to go, but it just hasn't happened yet. The metal bars underneath the futon are broken, so we put pieces of wood under the mattress to stop your butt from falling through. The fabric on the mattress is torn, so we flipped it over, and the rips are on the bottom. Definitely time for the futon to go.

I'm not holding on to it for sentimental reasons, just practical ones. I don't have anything else for visitors to sleep on, and it will be a lot of work to carry that thing up the stairs and out the door. If I *kept* it for sentimental reasons, that would be totally understandable. That futon has played a huge part in our youth ministry at Runway Ranch. A lot of teens have slept on that not-so-comfortable futon. Some were just hanging out, maybe part of a girls' or guys' night out, crashing at Runway Ranch as part of a youth event, but for others, it really was a home away from home. More than just a place to sleep, for some, it was a refuge in the middle of the night; for others, a quiet place to be alone; and for some, it was an escape from the harsh realities of their lives,

---

1 https://www.youtube.com/watch?v=gx2s02URGds

if only for one night. For others, that beat-up futon was a place to curl up and let the tears stream down their face until the sun rose in the morning and brought with it a brighter day.

For one of the teens, that futon was a hospital bed, a place to recover after having surgery to remove her tonsils. Her name was Tamara, and her family lived just down the road in the village of Val Rita. Tamara's mom couldn't get the time off work, so she asked if her daughter could stay at Runway Ranch for a few days. While she was there, a neighbor stopped by. I wasn't home. I can't remember if I had headed into town or was busy in the barn, but while I was out, our neighbor came to the door. Tamara was asleep on the couch, but she heard someone at the door, and she answered it. Tamara was in the middle of her goth phase, dressed in black with extra piercings. Her throat was too sore to speak, and she was living off Tylenol and popsicles. The whole meeting-the-neighbor thing was a blur to her. All she could remember was that someone came to the door. However, my neighbor thought it might be a good idea to give me a call. They said, "I stopped by today and, um… your um, daughter… maybe, answer the door. She um… didn't look very good."

It still makes me smirk to picture who my neighbor met at the door that day. An extra quiet, half asleep, goth girl, high on painkillers and purple popsicles.

We never considered making Runway Ranch more than just a home away from home for any of the teens, until Josh. Josh was probably 13 when he started coming to what was then The Living Fire youth group. He had been invited by a friend and had been coming to every Friday night activity and to church almost every Sunday for years. We liked Josh; he was a good kid. He could definitely keep up with the guys when it came to roughing around and did have to spend a Saturday afternoon patching up a wall at the church with one of the girls because they had crashed into it way too hard the night before, but he *really* was a good kid. One evening after youth group, Josh told me he probably wasn't coming back. Josh had been told by social services that he was not allowed to live with his dad, so he had been staying with his grandma. Staying at his grandma's house wasn't working out, and Josh's family was making arrangements for him to move in with his mom in the city. I could tell that Josh was upset. He hadn't lived with his mom since he was five. Josh was worried. He said his mom struggled with drug addiction and that it wasn't a good environment for him. I could tell that he didn't want to go. I didn't say anything that night. It took everything I had, except physically putting my hand over my mouth, not to tell him he could live at Runway Ranch with our family. It wasn't entirely my decision to make.

When teens would come and go, Tim wouldn't say much about it. That was temporary, but this would be different. It wouldn't be an overnight stay on the futon in the corner of the rec room. This was a potentially life-changing decision. I talked to Tim about Josh's situation. I told him I wanted to offer Josh a home. Tim was surprisingly OK with it. I was literally surprised. I expected him to talk me down, explain why it was a bad idea, tell me it wasn't my place to try and fix the situation, but he didn't do any of that. He asked me two questions, one; is he lazy? I didn't think so. And two, will he listen to you if you tell him to do something? I said he would.

I think Tim was looking out for me. He had taken on a new job flying for Sunwing and was based in Toronto. He had to be away from home a lot. He knew that if we allowed Josh to stay with us that I would be the one with the day-to-day responsibility of having another child in the house.

Before I talked to Josh, I talked to Benjamin. Victoria had already moved out. She was married at 18, and she and Kyle were living in Ottawa while they finished their schooling. Ben was only 14, and suddenly having an older brother could have been really hard on him. So, I wanted to know what he thought. I told Benjamin that we were thinking of offering Josh a place to live. I told him it might be difficult for him to have Josh around all the time and that I wanted to know what he thought before I decided. I don't know that I have ever been more proud of my son. He took a moment to think about it and then said, with the rawest honesty you can imagine, "It might be hard for me, Mom, but I think it would be good for him. You should ask Josh to stay here."

That Sunday, we offered Josh a home at Runway Ranch. I was very real with him. I told him that he might not like it, that it isn't always fun. He would need to be up at 6:30 AM every day to do chores with the boys before they caught the bus. I told him he would have to get a job and save money for college. I also told him that he would have a curfew just like Victoria did when she was at home and that he would have to keep going to youth group on Fridays and attend church with us every Sunday. I told him that he would have the same rules as the boys and would have to listen to Tim if Tim asked him to do anything. I wasn't trying to scare him off; I just wanted him to understand that living at Runway Ranch was much different than hanging out there for a youth event. Josh talked to his grandma, and I talked to his grandma. It was official; Josh was moving in. We built a wall in the rec room and converted what was once Tim's office space into a bedroom. Tim's massive wooden desk stayed in the room, and unless the wall comes down someday, that desk isn't going anywhere. It doesn't fit through the door.

We had told Josh that he could stay with us until he went away to college. We enjoyed having him there, and he was welcome to stay, but in the back of my mind, I thought that if things changed for his dad and Josh wanted to, then moving back with his dad was always an option. Until one day, it wasn't.

It was early on a Sunday morning when I got the call. Although Josh's aunt couldn't give him a place to stay, she still cared about him deeply and wanted to be the one to tell him. She said she would meet us at the church since we were on our way in. I don't think I said a word to Josh the whole ride to town. How could I pretend that everything was OK when it was not? Josh was in the back with the boys; it wasn't just another Sunday morning, but they didn't know that. Josh's aunt was in the church lobby when we came in. I stepped aside and let them talk. I couldn't hear what they were saying, but I knew and had no idea what to do next. Would he want me to comfort him? I just stood at the back of the church, feeling such uncertainty. Josh turned around, and we stood there looking straight into each other's eyes. He was telling me what happened without saying a word. I don't think either of us knew exactly what role we played in each other's lives. Did he want me to hold him?

Did he want me to comfort him? We never said a word. I walked over and put my arms around him. He wasn't a kid anymore. He was a young man, and he held on tight. He didn't cry; he just held on tight.

The next morning when I went downstairs to check on Josh, he was curled up in a ball beside his bed. He said he couldn't sleep; it didn't matter where he was, he couldn't get comfortable. Even his own bed didn't bring him any comfort. After Josh's dad died, Josh became withdrawn and spent much time in his room. Sometimes, it felt like all we could do was love him. We ensured that Josh knew he was surrounded by people who cared about him. I'd like to say that as time passed, things got back to normal, but I have a feeling that after you lose someone you love, you begin to live a new normal. Josh's new normal was us; he quickly became a full-time part of the Runway Ranch family, and we were blessed to have him.

While he was with us, his grades went from failing to above average. He once confessed to me that he was actually pretty smart, but he hadn't let anyone know that because he didn't want them to have high expectations. After seeing his new grades, I let him know that the secret was out. He was a smart kid. It was great having Josh around. He was a good friend for Ben and a good big brother to the younger boys.

In the last couple of months, before Josh went away to school, things changed. It was a rough time for both of us. Josh wasn't happy; he was easily irritated. He no longer wanted to help the boys with the chores and would complain and get angry about it. This was a side of Josh that I had never seen before. I remember one day in the spring when the snow was still on the ground. Josh was outside. I put on my snowsuit, hat, and mitts. I didn't know how long this conversation was going to take. We sat in the snowbank together and talked things out. It was actually a long conversation, but the end result was that Josh was turning eighteen and didn't want to follow anyone else's rules; he wanted to make his own decisions. I could understand where he was coming from. I told him it was normal to feel that way. It's a part of growing up to want to make your own decisions and do your own thing. But I also explained that within a family, rules are set in place for a reason, that in a few months, he would be headed off to college and would definitely experience the independence he was looking for.

Josh started spending the weekends at his grandma's place. He enjoyed the freedom of not having chores or a curfew, and a few weeks before he left for college, he moved back in with his grandma. We saw Josh a couple of times when he was in college, but it wasn't until he moved back to Kapuskasing many years later that it felt as if our relationship was restored.

Josh was the only student from the youth ministry that lived with us. Since then, several students have asked if they could stay, but I always said the same thing. If they needed a place for the night, I had a futon in the corner of the rec room. I wanted Runway Ranch to remain a place of refuge, somewhere the students could temporarily go when they needed to get away, and never again a place they felt they needed to get away from.

Connor took us up on the offer many times, not because he needed to get away but because he liked to hang out.

Connor was one of our youth students, but he was also a

good friend to the boys in their teenage years. He spent a lot of time at our house, which I didn't mind at all. At over 6 feet tall, Connor was kind of a friendly giant. He was quite the troublemaker at home and school, but at Runway Ranch, he was just a big guy with a big heart. We liked having him over; he always wanted to cook us breakfast on Saturday mornings, that was just a bonus. Connor walked into our house one day and randomly said, "When I'm at your house, I feel like I'm in a PG movie."

One day early in the summer, the guys had made plans for Connor to stay the weekend. He showed up with a backpack full of tomato soup cans. I told Connor he should call his dad to make sure it was OK for him to stay. A few minutes later, Connor handed me the phone because his dad wanted to talk to me. He told me it was OK for Connor to stay and that he would pick him up in September. Wait *what*? Had I heard that right? His dad said he would pick him up in September. I told Connor it probably wasn't a good idea for him to stay the whole summer but he could stay a couple of days and was welcome to come back whenever he wanted. Our old worn-out futon hosted Conner almost every weekend that summer.

I often think of that "if you give us this house" deal I made with God. Was the futon included in the deal? I think it was. "If you give us this house, I will…let teenagers sleep on the futon."

"Now to him who is able to do immeasurably more than all we ask or imagine, according to his power that is at work within us," Ephesians 3:20 NIV

43

Chapter 5

More Where That Came From

"I now have a mental sticky note that goes along with any creative idea that God gives me. The note reads, 'There's plenty more where that came from'"

~ *Sarah Jane.*

As a mom, I often have moments where all I want is for my kids to do what I tell them to, when I tell them to. None of this, "after the game," "when this video is over," "I'm just going to grab a snack first." They might as well just say what they really mean. "I'll do it, but you're gonna have to ask me ten times first." I wonder if God ever feels this way about me.

I was getting things ready for the Lindsay fall fair many years ago. The Lindsay fair was great. I liked to go and take Victoria and Benjamin to see all the animals. Tim liked to go and stock up on a variety of overpriced fudge. The best part was that if you had a float in the fall fair parade, then you could get into the fair for free. I was the children's ministry director at our church, and we were putting together a big float for the parade. I say big because the bigger the wagon, the more children and parents could hop on for a free ride into the fairgrounds.

Decorating this float was a very difficult task for me. The decorating itself was easy. I had plenty of help, lots of creative ideas, and a stack of materials to work with. The struggle was an internal one. What I was creating didn't line up with what God was asking me to create.

The summer program I had been running had a super cool *God Made the World* theme. We had lots of decorations that really made the theme come alive. I got some giant balloons and spent hours creating paper mâché planets that were painted and hung from the ceiling. I had decided to move this theme over to our fall fair parade float. However, I really felt like God was asking me to do something different. Something more powerful. Over a thousand people were going to see this float. It was definitely an opportunity to make an impact. Should I have made big signs with specific Bible verses or built a huge wooden cross? I don't know. I don't know because anytime I would get that little nudge here and there, like maybe God was trying to tell me something, I would dismiss it. I didn't want to hear it. I had my heart set on cotton ball clouds and paper mâché planets. I wasn't listening. I'm sure there have been plenty of times when God was trying to get my attention, but this was one of the few times I deliberately ignored that small voice in my head. I know we're not supposed to live in the past, but I often wonder what the float would have looked like if I had actually allowed God to design it. How influential it could have been. I know when the Spirit of God asks you to do something, He does it for a reason.

I woke up one night with a woman's name in my head. I didn't know her. I didn't remember ever hearing her name before, but I couldn't get it out of my head. The next morning, I told Tim about it. I still remembered the name, so I asked him if he knew her. He said he wasn't sure but that it might be the name of a lady that went to our church. He said I should've prayed for her, that maybe God put her name in my head for a reason. That Sunday, a lady stood up in church to say something. Tim leaned over and said I think that is the lady whose name was in your head a couple of nights ago. She had stood up to ask for prayer. She said that two nights ago, her son suffered a heart attack and was in the hospital. Two nights ago? That's the same night that God woke me up with her name in my head. Tim and I just looked at each other. I don't know exactly what he was thinking, but I was thinking, "Wow, this is unbelievably crazy." I learned my lesson. If God wakes you up in the middle of the night with a person's name in your head, pray for them! And that is exactly what I did the next time that it happened—only that time, I actually knew the person.

I was sleeping in my old bedroom at my parents' house. Tim and I were there for a visit. In the middle of the night, I woke up with my brother's name in my head, but this time it was different, more intense, a sit-up straight and gasp for air kind of wake-up call. I remembered what to do. If you wake up with someone's name in your head, pray for them. So, I did. I didn't know what to pray for, but I prayed. My brother's name is Timothy. I prayed, "Dear God, please help Timothy." What else could I pray? I didn't know what he needed prayer for, so "God, please help Timothy" was what I prayed.

The next morning, my brother Luke was sleeping in the spare room. That was really weird since he didn't live at home anymore. When my parents asked him why he was there, he said he wanted to talk to them before they headed to town. He didn't want them to see my brother Tim's truck, which had crashed and burned on the side of their road the night before. He wanted them to know that Timothy was OK. Later that day, my brother Timothy told us what happened. He had lost control of the truck, driven off the road, and hit the rock face. Timothy was knocked out, and the truck was on fire. He woke up just in time to escape through the smashed back window and run to the road before the truck exploded. Timothy described it like a scene from a movie; the entire truck lifted off the ground as it exploded into flames.

Timothy's near-death experience was happening at the same time God had placed the very intense, *pray for your brother* wake up call. As I said, when the Spirit of God asks you to do something, He does it for a reason.

When the kids were a little older, and we had moved to Kapuskasing, I occasionally needed a babysitter. It wasn't very often and not for long periods of time, but when I needed a babysitter, Jackie would help out. Jackie was one of the boys' Sunday school teachers. She wasn't working then, so she didn't mind stopping by occasionally if I had a meeting. One evening, Jackie stopped by to watch the kids. She was there for less than an hour. When it came time to pay her, I went to my room and pulled out a cash box I kept in the closet. I was running a photography business at the time, so I had plenty of cash on hand. I put the cash box on the bed and opened the lid to take out a $10 bill. There beside the ten-dollar bill was a one-hundred-dollar bill. I was getting pretty good at recognizing God's voice, and at that moment, he spoke to me. He said, "Give her the hundred dollar bill."

I know it was God and not me because that definitely wasn't my idea. I didn't mind being generous, but a hundred dollars an hour for babysitting seemed a little excessive. I held up the ten dollars in one hand and the one hundred dollars in the other hand. Unlike that time when God told me to change out the fall fair float theme, and I completely ignored him, this time, I listened. I put the ten-dollar bill back in the cash box and gave Jackie the one-hundred-dollar bill. I said, "God told me to give you this." Her response is why I should always listen when God speaks. She started to cry, and as she hugged me, she said, "Thank you so much; I really needed this. Now I can pay my hydro bill." I had no idea that Jackie was struggling financially. But God did. He always knows.

I was starting to recognize more and more the voice of God in my life, but just like my kids, when I would give them a job to do, I didn't always listen right away. It's not that I'm a fan of procrastination. I'm usually a 'just get it done' kind of person, especially in youth ministry. When it came to hearing God's voice and taking action, I probably needed a lesson on timing.

There's a spot on the highway between Kapuskasing and Silver Birches camp. It's called the Arctic Watershed. It's a rest stop where travelers can pull over. There's a sign there that says welcome to the Arctic Watershed. This marks the line across the map where all the rivers begin to flow north into the Arctic Ocean. I'd passed this spot on the highway a hundred times before and never really thought anything of it.

One day as I was driving by to pick up the teens from youth

camp, an idea crossed my mind—more like an inspirational message, actually. After spending a week at youth camp, our students always felt encouraged, uplifted, on a spiritual high. For most of them, a restoration had occurred in their relationship with God. They were empowered. For some, it was a life-changing week, but for others, it was a mountaintop experience that they would have a hard time holding onto once they returned home. The Arctic Watershed would be the perfect place to stop and talk about not turning back in their relationship with God. This is exactly what God was asking me to do, to stop at the Arctic watershed sign on my way back and encourage the students to keep moving forward no matter what obstacles they encountered.

We crammed their over-packed luggage into the vehicle and headed back to Kapuskasing. Kids were covered with sleeping bags and pillows. As we approached the Watershed rest stop, I started thinking of excuses. We probably shouldn't stop because parents will be waiting, or I'll have to repack this overloaded vehicle if we get out. I didn't stop. I didn't say a word to anyone about it. I just drove by the rest stop as if it wasn't even there. The next year, I did the exact same thing. I packed up the youth at camp with an unexplainable feeling that I should stop at the Arctic Watershed and share the message laid on my heart the year before. I didn't. I just drove right by again. Apparently, what I felt was an assignment from God had no expiry date, because there I was, one more year later, driving by the Arctic Watershed on my way to pick up youth at camp when God said, "You should stop there on the way back and share that message." I could still remember the message as if he put it in my heart that very day. We packed up the youth at camp just like we always did, with a crazy amount of luggage everywhere, and headed out on the highway. A passion for this message began to well up inside of me. I wasn't going to let another year go by without doing what I knew God was asking me to do.

I slowed down and turned off at the Watershed. The sign was on top of the hill. As we drove up the hill, the teens had questions about where we were stopping and why. We all got out of the vehicles and stood around the "from here all waters flow north" sign. I explained what that meant and went on to share with the youth the message that God had laid on my heart. I told them it was two years overdue, but there it was. The idea of leaving the past in the past and moving forward in their relationship with God must have hit home. I wasn't expecting the students to be as passionate about receiving the message as I was about giving it, but I could tell from their response that this had a powerful impact on them.

After we talked, we prayed together. It was an emotional time for some of the students. One of the young men looked up with tears in his eyes. He looked at me and nodded as if to say, "I get it." He might have got it a whole lot earlier if I had done what God said *when* he said. I really did need to work on my timing; maybe practice what I tell my kids about doing what you're told when you're told to do it. It had taken me three trips to camp to finally share the watershed message with the teens. That's not the only time I held onto something God had asked me to share.

Part of running youth ministry was speaking to the older teens every Friday night about important life lessons, inspirational messages, and creative devotions, all based on biblical truths. For a little while, I struggled to find something that I really felt passionate about and wanted to teach a series on. That's not actually true; I did have one really awesome idea that I couldn't wait to preach on. It was one of those God-inspired ideas that comes with all the extras.

The message was called The Big Picture. It was all about God having a bigger plan than what we can see—how the hard things we sometimes go through are not the end of the story, that God can take the ugly times and make something beautiful come out of them. This idea came fully stocked with an Art Attack intro video and a puzzle piece for every student. The puzzle pieces would fit into a large picture of Jesus holding up a struggling teenager displayed at the front of the room. God had blessed me with this idea, and it was good. I was passionate about it. So passionate that I decided to save it.

I know that doesn't make sense, but I hosted larger youth events with up to a hundred teens throughout the year, and I really wanted to share something great at the next sectional youth event. The big-picture message was great, so I saved it and filed it in the back of my mind for another time. I thought that was a good plan, but I was wrong. Week to week, I was struggling to find something I really thought would help the students, motivate them, and encourage them. It was as if I had writer's block, but I wasn't writing. I guess it was preacher's block. Is that a thing?

Meanwhile I had that very specific Big Picture message that God had laid on my heart tucked away for another time. At the next sectional youth event that I hosted, I preached The Big Picture. It was good, really seemed to pack a punch for the students, just like I had anticipated.

In the weeks following, I had no problem planning lessons, messages, and devotions. My mind was flooded with good ideas. I learned my lesson. I never should have filed away The Big Picture. I should have preached it. I should have used the idea that God had given me when he gave it to me and not six months later.

My mistake reminds me of the story in the Bible, Matthew 25:14-30. There was a man who was going away. He entrusted gold coins to three of his servants. The first two servants invested the coins and made a profit. The third servant hid the coins in the ground. When the man returned, he blessed the servants who had made a profit but kicked out the third servant. He took the gold coins from him and gave them to the first servant.

The point is, if you use what God gives you, He will trust you with even more. I now have a mental sticky note that goes along with any creative idea God gives me. The note reads, "There's plenty more where that came from."

One of my boys came into my room the other day and told me he had an idea for me to preach to the youth. I told him that it was his idea and he should preach it. He said, and I quote, "I'm not the youth pastor." I said maybe you could be. He said, "Nah, this is the only message I have." I confidently told him that if God had given him that message that he should use it and see what happens next. He shouldn't bury it away like the coins in the story; he should share it. If he does, he may discover plenty more where that came from.

Whether it's a creative message, a plan for a fall fair parade float, an overpaid babysitter, or a midnight wake-up call with someone's name in your head, when God asks you to do something, He does it for a reason.

"His master replied, 'Well done, good and faithful servant! You have been faithful with a few things; I will put you in charge of many things. Come and share your master's happiness!'"

Matthew 25:21

Chapter 6

Not *Just* a Volunteer

"Our ministries are stronger, more effective, and probably a whole lot more fun because of the dedicated, talented, and sometimes crazy people who show up and make things happen."

~Sarah Jane

He stood at the front of the room and said, "Students, you're in the auditorium here with our special guests. Volunteers, you're in the side room. Main youth leaders, you're with me." Seemed like an easy way to break up the room, a simple way of letting everyone know where they should be, but it wasn't simple for me. I was the main youth leader for our group, but unlike the other main youth leaders in the room, I was a volunteer. In the past, I'd always gone with the volunteers. The sessions were great, always inspirational, but not designed for the main youth pastor. This time I gathered up that tiny bit of rebel I had in me and walked right past the side room where the volunteers were meeting.

In my church, I was the youth pastor. Volunteer or not, I was responsible for our students. Dividing leaders based on whether or not they are paid for their job didn't sit well with me. Paycheque or no paycheque didn't make a difference. This was my job, and I'd never given less than 100% just because I wasn't on the payroll.

There were no formal introductions in the room, but we all said our hellos and took our seats. It was a casual, relaxed atmosphere. The same gentleman that had divided the groups was leading our session. He was a pretty popular guy and needed no introduction. I recognized him, but he understandably didn't recognize me. He asked me what my name was and where I was from. "I'm Sarah, and I am from Kapuskasing." He said, "Kapuskasing? I didn't know that we had a youth leader in Kapuskasing." He didn't know because I wasn't on staff. Having a volunteer position meant my name wasn't on any list that would have crossed his desk. I told him I volunteered to run the youth ministry, and this is what he said: "Oh, you're just a volunteer."

Really? Just a volunteer. I've never been crazy about the expression "just a volunteer." The word "just" makes it sound like something is missing, as if being a volunteer and not a staff member somehow makes me less of a leader. I brushed it off. I was sure he hadn't meant that I was "just" a volunteer, but by the end of the session, I realized that that was exactly what he meant. After going through parts of his session, he would stop and look at me and repeat himself. At one point, after making an analogy about students and some biblical references, he actually said out loud that he would repeat himself for me because, as a volunteer, I probably hadn't come across that scenario. I thought, sure, it doesn't hurt to say it twice, but it's totally unnecessary. I was a volunteer, not a rookie. I'd been to Bible college and had at least 10 years of child and youth ministry experience. I wasn't *just* a volunteer. As I said, this was my job, regardless of whether or not it came with a pay stub.

I was at my parents' place one weekend. It's about 4 hours from home. Well, 3 1/2 hours now that the kids are grown. We no longer need all those side-of-the-road pee breaks. I told my parents I needed to head home because I was hosting a youth event that week. My dad said, "Maybe someone else can do it; you're just a volunteer, right?" There's something you need to know about my dad. He's an amazing guy, super supportive. Both my dad and my mom have always believed in me and made me feel like I could do anything I put my mind to. My dad was proud of the work I did in youth ministry, and I knew it. That's why his comment took me by surprise. I know he wanted me to stay, but there is no way he actually thought I would ditch the youth event I had been planning for months because I was *only* a volunteer. This was my job, and I took it seriously.

Sometime later, I was talking to my brother. I told him I had to go, that I had to go to work. That's what I called it—work—because that's what it was. He said, "What, you have a job now?" I reminded him that I worked at the church as the youth director and had for over 10 years. He said, "Oh, yeah, that; I thought you meant a real job." Technically, he was right; it wasn't a real job, as it didn't come with a T4 slip at the end of the year. But it was real to me, and I loved it. That volunteer position gave me an opportunity to do what I always felt God was calling me to do.

As a youth pastor, I've worked with a load of volunteers, both within the church and in the community. I've never thought of anyone as *just* a volunteer. Our ministries are stronger, more effective, and probably a whole lot more fun because of the dedicated, talented, and sometimes crazy people who show up and make things happen.

The students in our youth programs were given plenty of opportunities to volunteer. They were learning about serving others and making a difference when I introduced them to Go Mad. "What's a Mad night?" the students would ask. A Go Mad night was a new event I was starting with the teens. It was all about volunteering. I wanted to allow the teens to really live out some of the lessons that they had been learning on Friday nights. I wanted to give them a chance to go out in the world and "make a difference," or as we called it, Go M.A.D. On a Go Mad night, the students would be divided into smaller groups and head out into the community to lend a hand. One group set up a small library at a local school, while another volunteered to sort cans at the food bank. Sometimes, they babysat for single moms or shoveled snow for the elderly. At Christmas, they sang carols at Walmart while collecting food for hungry families. Planning activities that would allow the students.to volunteer, to help others with nothing in return, had always been a part of leading youth ministry.

The high school youth group was called Rooted. One Go Mad night, the Rooted students created what is now known in Kapuskasing as the community dinner. We called it the pop-up kitchen. It all started with a lesson and a challenge. The lesson was found in the Bible in Matthew 25. It was a lesson about helping others. This lesson was followed by a challenge. The teens were divided into groups of 3 or 4 and asked to think about a need in the community. Then they were asked to create an event that we could do as a group to meet that need. I told them to be as creative as they wanted and not to let their ideas be limited by the size of our group or the size of our bank account. I've learned never to underestimate the power of a teenager's imagination. I asked them to be creative, and they did not disappoint.

This was more than a challenge for the teens. It was a competition. I told the groups we would take the winning idea and make it happen. I gathered up the papers with each group's ideas on them and took them home with me. Later that night, I went through the papers and saw an underlying theme. Almost every group had noticed families in our community that needed proper meals. Every group rose to the challenge of the Go Mad competition, but one group had really put their creative thinking caps on. This was their idea. We should put on a free dinner for those in need, but not just a dinner: a sit-down dining experience. Not just a dining experience but a place to shop for free clothing while they wait to be served. Not just free clothing but free Bibles and Christian magazines as well.

Ladies and gentlemen, we had a winner. I messaged the students to let them know the winning idea and that we would plan it at our next Go Mad night, and plan it we did! We found a chef. Her name was Nicky. Nicky had helped with fundraising dinners in the past. Some of the students got together with Nicky to plan a menu and figure out how much money we would need. Other students volunteered to take letters around town asking for donations. Others collected Bibles from a gentleman in our church who was connected with the Gideons. We chose a date, sent out posters, and made a Facebook post.

The night of the dinner, everything the students had imagined in their Go Mad challenge had become a reality. Everything was perfect, as long as you couldn't see behind the scenes. Behind the scenes, things were a little messy. OK, a whole lot messy. Our church was under construction, so we had booked the high school cafeteria for the dinner. Unfortunately, a snowstorm made it a school snow day, and they had to cancel our booking. Nicky arranged to cook the meal at her house. The teens drove to the church with loaded pots, pans, roasters, and slow cookers. I contacted the radio station, and they announced a last-minute change of location. We called in the church maintenance guy to help us with the ever-blowing fuses where the slow cookers and roasting pans were plugged in. The students quickly cleared away the chairs in the church and brought the tables out of storage. The center of the room had become a sit-down restaurant, complete with tablecloths and candy favors on each plate. Visitors could shop for free clothing donated from Walmart or soap and cleaning supplies donated from Shoppers Drug Mart. They could even pick up a new toothbrush courtesy of a local dentist.

Nicky and I had given a crash course on serving, and our visitors were treated to a dining experience complete with yes, sir and yes, ma'am. Our first dinner served only 30 people, but the students were not disappointed. They had nothing to compare it to and had no idea how many people to expect. The dinner was a hit. We decided that we would do it again whenever we had enough money. There was no specific time frame, just whenever we could; that led us to call it a pop-up kitchen. The more pop-up kitchens we did, the more guests started coming out.

While Nicky was stirring up things in the kitchen, God was stirring up things in the hearts of the people in our church. Adults began asking to volunteer, and we appreciated the help. One couple in our church asked to cover the cost of the dinners so that we could make it a monthly event. When the construction on the kitchen was complete, the students would come after school on the last Friday of every month to set up tables, chop vegetables, make salads and juice, and set out donated clothes to give away. The Go Mad challenge would become a reality again.

It's been seven years since that group of 12 teen volunteers created the pop-up kitchen, now known as the community dinner. The dinner has become a staple in our community and part of the church's annual budget. They now have an amazing chef and a first-class group of kitchen volunteers that make 120 free meals at the end of each month. Our teens served at every community dinner until Covid hit, and the dinners were switched to takeout. The idea was that the students would go make a difference, and they did!

When the students were serving the community dinner, we would always take a few minutes first and go over that Bible lesson that inspired us in the first place. Yes, the same lesson the last Friday of every month. I may have put a new spin on it occasionally, but the message was the same. Eventually, I could call on almost any student in the room, tell them it was their turn to do the lesson, and they could do it from memory. When new teens would come out to help serve, they would hear all about Matthew 25:40, where a king had an inheritance prepared for the people who fed him when he was hungry, who gave him something to drink when he was thirsty, who took him in when he was a stranger and visited him when he was sick or in prison. The king's people were totally confused and asked, "When did we do that? We don't remember doing any of those things for you." The king replied, "Truly, I tell you, whatever you did for one of the least of these brothers and sisters of mine, you did for me."

The teens were learning that serving others is a way of serving God. And those teens were definitely serving. They volunteered in different ministries at the church, on mission trips, Go Mad nights, and community events. Keeping track of how much a person volunteered to help out was never really important, not until the students started collecting community hours for school. They needed 40 hours of volunteer work to graduate. I always signed off on community hours when students volunteered, but I didn't always want to. It was better to see the teams from Rooted youth helping out because they wanted to and not because they got something out of it. Over the years, I was pleasantly surprised at how many of our students didn't care about community hours; they collected them, but the 40-hour requirement never seemed to limit them. I have a notebook with a column for names and a column to add up community hours for each student. There are over 40 names on the list, but only once has someone said they weren't coming to volunteer because they already had their hours. Several of the Rooted students who have over 100 hours are still volunteering. I continuously thank them and tell them what a good job they're doing, but I still wonder if these students have any idea just how valuable their volunteer work is. They are more than "just" a volunteer. They are individuals who are serving others and making a difference.

The king replies by saying, 'Truly I tell you, whatever you did for one of the least of these brothers and sisters of mine, you did for me.' Matthew 25:40 NIV

Chapter 7

Spinning Mind

"I heard a very clear voice in my head say, 'because you won't stay still long enough during the day' Bam! That was powerful."

Originally, I titled this book "Inside The *Twisted* Mind Of A Volunteer Youth Leader." I later changed it to *Spinning* Mind because twisted mind sounded a little too Joker from Batman, kind of creepy. Rest assured, I don't have a creepy joker kind of twisted mind, but when I visualize what's going on in my head at any given time, it slightly resembles a mini tornado. Thoughts are flying around; I'm planning, organizing, scheduling, making lists on my mental notepad, replanning, reorganizing, rescheduling, and scratching things off that same mental notepad. It's a non-stop whirlwind of thoughts, a mental tornado. And that is where the twisted mind of a volunteer youth leader came from.

The Spinning Mind

You would think I would want to turn it off, make a stop, clear my head, but no. I thrive in this kind of environment. It's not unorganized or chaotic, it's just an endless flow of thoughts moving through my mind, and for me, it's a three-step process. You think it, you plan it, you make it happen. I do things. I'm a doer. I don't know if that's a real word, but that's what I am, and it works for me. You know what doesn't work for me? Staying still. I've never been good at that.

Tim had some travel perks through his work, and he took me on a vacation to Cuba. The resort was incredible, the food was amazing, perfect sandy beaches with an aqua-coloured ocean. The ultimate relaxation atmosphere, but not for me. I'd never been on vacation before, not like this. Anytime we had been away before, it always felt like taking care of the family but somewhere other than home. This was different. There were no kids to care for, no meals to make, and honestly, nothing to do but relax. Relaxing meant not thinking, not planning, and not making things happen. I am not wired that way.

The first morning at the resort, we headed to the beach, applied sunscreen, and made ourselves comfortable on some reclining lounge chairs. Tim pulled his hat down over his face and closed his eyes. After a minute of silence, I was ready to go. "Wanna walk on the beach?" I asked. "No, I just want to relax," was his reply. One minute later: "Wanna swim in the ocean?" "Nope, I just want to relax. Try it; just lay there and close your eyes." I tried; it was a no-go. If doing nothing was relaxing, then relaxing was boring. I couldn't do it. Eventually, I headed back to the room to grab my camera. I joined Tim back on the lounge chairs and began taking snapshots. A snapshot of the ocean, a snapshot of a palm tree, a snapshot of Tim sleeping, a snapshot of my toes in the sand. I'd photograph anything as long as it meant that I didn't have to sit there and do nothing.

The next day I had a plan. It was a book, actually. I don't read books, not normally, but I had a student who was struggling with a serious case of depression, and a pastor friend lent me a book about understanding depression. I had thrown it in my bag before we left. Not exactly poolside entertainment, but while Tim slept by the pool, I expanded my knowledge of depression and anxiety. It took a couple of days to adapt to my surroundings and allow myself, or should I say, to force myself to take a time out.

Today, we would call it taking a mental health day. I know that taking time to relax and recharge is important. I'm just not very good at it.

Several years ago, I took a group of students to Thunder Bay for a week-long mission trip. Planning a trip of any kind requires preparation but one where the cars are loaded with teenagers, even more so. Having all the details lined up ahead of time was super important to me. I was connected with Jessica from the Centre in Thunder Bay. She was my contact person. We messaged back-and-forth several times to arrange for my group to spend the week volunteering at the Centre and helping in her community. As the trip got closer, there were more and more details to finalize, but Jessica got harder and harder to get ahold of. I tried to be understanding, knowing how much responsibility she had. She must've been extremely busy. I have to confess that as the days went on and the details of our trip were not final-ized, I was growing impatient. I would call the office, but Jessica was never available. "I am sorry, but she's out of the office." "She's down by the river today." "She's gone on a hiking trip today." "You'll have to call her back; she's taking a quiet day on the mountain side." No joking; this was the response I got from her office.

I didn't get it. How could she take time off to sit by the river when she hadn't returned her emails yet? Why would she take time off to hike up a mountain when she hadn't finished making arrangements for the trip? The truth is, she wasn't taking time off. She was taking a time out. After getting to know Jessica during the mission trip, I had a better idea of what was really going on. Jessica's relationship with God was extremely important to her. She wanted every decision she made in ministry to be guided by the Holy Spirit, so she scheduled alone time with God. One-on-one quality God time by the river, on the hiking trail, or up the mountain.

You would think, being a pastor, that I would have been a little less judgmental when it came to someone wanting to spend some alone time with God. I mean, Jesus did the same thing, so it must not be a bad idea.

It's been one of the most familiar slogans in youth ministry over the past 20 years. WWJD. What would Jesus do? Christians quoted it; they wore it on their wristbands, printed it on their T-shirts, and stuck it to the bumpers of their cars. Others used WWJD as a punchline for a joke or a catchphrase for sitcoms. Still, others mocked the saying with funny videos or memes. But there is a reason why WWJD has been a trending expression over the years, and that's because it's a legit question. What *would* Jesus do, or more specifically, in the case of taking a time out, what *did* Jesus do? He spent alone time with God; that's what he did.

When Jesus had a big decision to make like when he chose the 12 disciples, He first took a time out. He actually spent the entire night praying on the mountainside. When the disciples had a long stressful day, Jesus told them that they also needed a time out. He said, "...Come with me by yourselves to a quiet place and get some rest" (Mark 6:31 NIV). When Jesus spent the day surrounded by a crowd, healing the sick and feeding the hungry, he must have been exhausted. What did he do? He took a time-out. Jesus headed up the mountain again for some much-needed alone time with God.

This is exactly what Jessica from the Centre was doing. She wasn't avoiding my calls or neglecting my emails; she was busy. Busy spending alone time with God.

I've preached it many times myself—the importance of being alone with God. One night, I had a conviction that I needed to practice what I preached. It wasn't unusual for me to wake up with a mind full of creative thoughts. I often prayed about things before I went to sleep, and God would answer my prayers in my dreams. If I was working on a message, I would wake up with pages of truly inspired words in my heart. If I was preparing a lesson or putting together a series, I would get a ton of ideas in the middle of the night.

During the Covid pandemic, I was planning a Christmas event, but I was drained. The guidelines were strict, and working around the mandates was really taking its toll on me. I was trying to organize a no-contact Christmas event, and I had used up the last drop of my creative juices. I woke up from a dream in the middle of the night. I had dreamt the entire Christmas event: the food, the message, the games, right down to the ugly Christmas sweater decorating competition! All I had to do now was bring it to life. God had blessed me with a vision, and I was extremely thankful for it. There were other times, however, when I had awakened in the middle of the night with a mini tornado of thoughts spinning in my head, and I wasn't thankful. I just wanted to sleep, but I found myself putting notes in my phone of creative ideas God was throwing at me.

The convicting realization that I needed to practice what I preached about spending time with God came around 3 am. It was another inspirational wake-up call of creative ideas, but this time, I prayed, "God, why? I love that you do this, but why at 3 AM????" I heard a very clear voice in my head say, "Because you won't stay still long enough during the day." Bam! That was powerful. It was a convicting realization that I needed to spend some alone time with God. I had no problem finding time to pray. I prayed in the car while I drove down the road. I prayed at the sink when I did the dishes; I even prayed in the shower. But I didn't set aside quiet time to listen for answers. If I wanted my youth ministry to be the best that it could be, and if I wanted a full night's sleep, I needed to set aside quiet time with God during the day. A relaxing, recharging timeout where I could hear God's voice over and above the mini tornado spinning in the mind of this volunteer youth leader.

Then, because so many people were coming and going that they did not even have a chance to eat, he said to them, "Come with me by yourselves to a quiet place and get some rest."

Mark 6:31 NIV

Chapter 8

I Like Your Focus

"Not praying or doing Bible lessons at youth events is like having a birthday party for someone and refusing to invite them."

~Sarah Jane

I was sitting in the eye doctor's chair, looking into a big silver binocular-shaped machine covered with spinning charts, levers, and gadgets. The doctor moved the gadgets back and forth. He got me to close one eye and then the other. It only took a few minutes before he said, "I see the problem; you're going to need glasses."

A few weeks earlier, I had been on vacation, and in my spare time, I entertained myself with Sudoku puzzles. Whenever I worked on a puzzle, I would get a dull ache behind my eyes. The doctor said I wouldn't need glasses immediately, but within the year, I would need to pick up a pair. He said not to get anything expensive, just buy a cheap pair off the rack at a dollar store. The year went by, and my eyes were fine. In fact, it was three years before I needed to take the doctor's advice. The dull ache was back, but it expanded beyond Sudoku puzzles. Any time that I read or wrote or played on my phone for too long, my eyes would tell me that it was time to listen to the doctor. The next time I was at a dollar store, I checked out the glasses, and even tried on a few pairs. I put on one pair, picked up a chocolate bar, and tried to read the fine print on the back of the wrapper. It worked; I could focus. I still didn't buy the glasses, but I did buy the chocolate bar. A couple of weeks later, I went back and picked up a pair of small frame, +1, leopard print glasses because being able to focus is important.

In youth ministry, that is exactly what I needed to do: focus. Games were fun, cool activities brought more kids out, field trips were exciting, and snacks always made things better, but the real focus needed to be on Jesus.

After leading a volunteer meeting to discuss our upcoming plans for children's ministry, one of the older teen guys saw me in the parking lot and said, "I really like your focus." I probably said something along the lines of "cool, thank you, and thanks for your help." I was impressed with him. When I got home, I told Tim about the student that really paid attention in the meeting. I told him that he hadn't just paid attention to the activities and the schedule but to the purpose of our children's ministry. When I told Tim that this guy had liked my focus, Tim laughed and said, "He was probably just trying to tell you that he liked your car." I had to work that out in my head. It only took a second to realize that Tim was right. I had a new car. It was a gold-coloured Ford Focus.

At one point, after I made the move to youth ministry, I decided that for a little while, we would focus on getting our community youth into church. I wanted to see the teens who hung out on Friday nights hang out on Sunday mornings, too. I wanted them to hear the lead pastor preach, sing praise and worship songs, and spend time with the rest of the church family. I focused on it. I added church to the monthly schedule, included an invite with Friday's announcements, and when I said goodbye to the students, I would make sure to say, "See you on Sunday," even if they had never come to church before.

I also tried praying kids into church, asking God to send them. When I was still overseeing the children's ministry, I wanted to see at least twenty kids each week. Before the kids were dismissed to go to children's programming, I would count them. I would count the kids sitting down, the kids standing on the pews, and the kids rolling around underneath them. We had a lot of community kids that came without their parents. Church looked a little crazy until the kids left for classes. One day I only counted 17 kids. I began to pray, "God, please send three more kids." After I prayed, a little guy with his two older sisters walked up the aisle. Another Sunday, I noticed that one of our regular teens wasn't there. I prayed that God would send her. A few minutes later, she came in and sat with the other teens at the front of the church. She was wearing her pajamas and carrying a pillow and a stuffed animal under her arm. She had been at a sleepover at her friend's house the night before and wasn't planning on coming to church. After she left her friend's house in the morning, she had a strong feeling that she needed to be in church, so she walked there, pillow, PJs and all.

The youth ministry focus was on getting teens to church. And it worked! At first, they began filling up the second row, then the second *and* third row, and eventually, there were so many teens that they didn't want to come in late because they would have to sit in the front row.

Another time, the focus of youth ministry was team building. The students in the youth group would see each other on Friday nights but weren't really friends outside of the church. I focused on building relationships between the teens, teaching them to love one another. We focused on Bible verses about encouraging each other in their faith, working together, and helping each other. We use the ropes course that Tim had built in the backyard at the farm to practice trust falls and help each other over the climbing wall.

The more we focused on team building, the tighter the team got. They started hanging out at each other's houses, walking to school together, having sleepovers on Saturday nights, and showing up together on Sundays. Almost everyone in the group went to the same school, and they started eating lunch together at the same table. It seemed like the ideal situation until I realized this group was too tight. They stopped hanging out with other people. They no longer had different groups of friends. They were content to just hang out with each other. They stopped bringing friends to youth group. When I would say, "Hey, bring a friend with you next week," they would just tell me that all their friends were already there. I told myself it was time to start a new focus; outreach.

As I would switch from one focus to another, I had to remind myself that more than helping the teens focus on where they were on a Sunday morning, more than helping them focus on building each other up, more than helping them focus on reaching others, it was my job to help them focus on their relationship with Jesus. Above all else, that needed to be my ministry focus. The Bible teaches that if we seek him first, if we focus on him, then He will take care of the rest. If I really wanted youth ministry to have a powerful impact on the lives of the teens that I worked with, then above anything else, the focus needed to be on Jesus. I remember telling our students and leaders that not praying or doing Bible lessons at youth events is like having a birthday party for someone and refusing to invite them.

I decided a few years ago to get my motorcycle license. I got a bike. Tim came home with a 2003 black Suzuki Marauder. It was a gift for our wedding anniversary. I started practicing in the yard. I practice switching gears and turning back and forth between pylons in the driveway. I practiced coming to a stop and not stalling when I took off again. I could do all of these things, but there was one thing I could not do. I could not make a sharp turn. All I wanted to be able to do was go out the end of my driveway, turn around, and  come back on the other side. But I couldn't make the turn. I couldn't seem to make it past the mailbox. I would have three choices; hit the mailbox, hit the ditch, or stop the bike, push it back out and try again. I chose option number three over and over again.

Finally, I decided that I was going to make this happen. I was going out one side of the driveway and back in the other. I gave myself a pep talk and headed out of the yard. As I turned to come back into the driveway, I was looking right at the mailbox. It was getting closer and closer. All I had to do was go around it, just turn the bike a little bit sharper. And then it happened, mailbox versus motorcycle. The mailbox won. It was the first time I went down on my bike. A few weeks later, I took the motorcycle training course. We did all the prep work, and then they put us on the bikes. The first thing the instructor did was set up the pylons in a tiny little circle. He instructed us to enter the circle, do a sharp turn, and come back out where we had gone in. Seriously, the first thing is a sharp turn? I tried, but nope, wasn't going to happen. I came out on the wrong side of the circle every time.

The next day the instructor set up all of the different parts of the course that we needed to complete in order to pass the exam. The more I practiced, the easier things got. I was able to do all of the requirements except one. We needed to enter a sharp turn with pylons on either side, complete the turn, and exit the pylons at the other end. When we were on break, the instructor asked me how I was doing. I said I was struggling with the sharp turn. He said that he had noticed and that he had some advice for me. What he said next was profound. He pointed at the exit of the sharp turn. "If that is where you want to be, then you need to look over there." He went on to say, "Don't look at where you're going; turn your head and look at where you want to be." Wow, instructor dude, that's not a riding lesson; that's a life lesson. This is why I couldn't turn away from the mailbox, because it was the very thing I was focusing on. Lesson learned. Don't look at the mailbox in front of you; turn your head and look at where you want to be.

I got up to the line, put the bike in gear, turned my head, and looked at where I wanted to be. There stuck in the grass at the other end of the pylons was a Tim Hortons bag. I thought, that's it; that's where I need to be. I let go of the clutch, and I focused on that Tim Hortons bag. I did not take my eyes off it. I made the corner, and not just that one time. I would line up, turn my head, look at the Tim Hortons bag, and make the corner, line back up, turn my head, look at the Tim Hortons bag, and make the corner, over and over. After we had finished practicing, we broke for lunch. When we returned to do the exam, someone had cleaned up the parking lot, or the wind blew really hard because the Tim Hortons bag was gone. I told myself that I could handle this, that I knew what to do. I just had to remember not to look at the pylons in front of me but to turn my head and focus on where I wanted to be.

In youth ministry, I wanted our students to be rooted in God. This inspired me to change the name of our group from The Living Fire to Rooted. We found a Rooted logo and ordered some really cool Rooted shirts. I told the students that I wanted their roots to be dug down so deep in Jesus that nothing and no one could come between them and their relationship with Him. So rooted that if things ever got bad, the storms of life would not blow them away.

The focus was to see them stay connected to Jesus. I told the students about a video where a stunt man had done a bungee jump with phone books. He had taken two large phone books and overlapped the pages one at a time. When the two phone books were completely overlapped, the stunt man cut the bungee rope and put it back together with only the phone books holding the two pieces of rope together. The overlapped pages of the phone books held the ropes together when he jumped.

That is what I wanted for the teens. That is how connected, how Rooted I wanted them to be in their relationship with God. From the wisdom of a motorcycle instructor, I learned that if that is where we wanted the teens to be, then that is what I would need to focus on.

Encouraging the teens to be in church on Sunday was a good idea. Teaching them to love one another and build each other up was important. Giving them the tools they needed to share the love of God with others was a huge part of youth ministry. But even more importantly, I needed to put on those small-rimmed, leopard-print glasses and ensure the youth ministry was always focused on Jesus.

But seek first his kingdom and his righteousness, and all these things will be given to you as well.

Matt 6:33 NIV

Chapter 9

Dangling the Carrot

"Maybe God was kick-starting something that I couldn't see."
~Sarah Jane

I sat at my computer with the arrow scrolling back and forth across the send button. Why was I so emotional? Pastor Jason was easy to talk to. Telling him what was on my mind had never been difficult, so why was I having a hard time with this? It was just a question, but it was one I never saw myself asking. It's not that I was being shy; it had just never seemed necessary to ask about it. I didn't understand why this question was so heavy on my heart, but I had experienced this feeling of urgency before and recognized that God was telling me that it was time. It was one simple question, so why was it so hard?

I reread the message: "Hey, Pastor, do you think that at some point, the church could make my job a paid position?"

Asking this question wasn't only making me a little emotional, but it was messing with my mind. I felt guilty, selfish, and even greedy for asking about money that would otherwise be used for ministry. I wasn't ungrateful for years of opportunity to work with the teens, not at all, but I thought it might look like I was. Despite these thoughts spinning in my mind, I knew that sending the question was the right thing to do, that when God asks you to do something, He does it for a reason.

I'd been in a similar situation before, but the last time was easier. I wasn't emotional, and it hadn't messed with my head. That was several years before we moved to Kapuskasing. When I was running the children's ministry in Lindsay, Tim told me I should ask about getting paid for some of the work I was doing. Tim was a flight instructor at a small airport and wasn't making very much money. He said, "It doesn't make sense that you're volunteering at the church, but I am paying off your student loan." It was true; it didn't make sense. I had been to Bible College for my biblical certificate and was now working at the church for free. I asked the pastor what he thought about the church paying off my student loan. He asked what the payment was. I said, "Eighty dollars a month." The pastor kind of chuckled. "Eighty dollars a month, that's it?" He said, "Yes, of course, we can do it; that's peanuts for what you do around here." I had a feeling that the conversation would go a little differently this time around.

I never did hear back from Pastor Jason, and the next time I saw him, I didn't want to bring it up. Not because I wasn't thinking about it. I definitely was. I was thinking, *why did I send that message?* It was like an after-the-fact facepalm moment. I didn't care if I got paid. I never cared about that. So why did I ask? I did youth ministry because I wanted to, because I felt that God had called me to it, and because I was passionate about it. But I also felt God was leading me to ask that question; was the church willing to pay me? So, there it was; we weren't talking about it, but it was out there.

Actually, the question had already been out there. Not because I asked but because other people had. For two years, a lady in our church stood up at the annual business meeting and asked if the church was considering putting me on the payroll. We also had someone come into a pastor's office and ask the same thing. The reply was always the same; "That's something we should look into."

I appreciated the gesture. As far as I was concerned, having people say that I deserved to be paid was all the payment that I needed. My hard work had not gone unnoticed. People appreciated what I was doing with the teens. That brought more satisfaction than a paycheque ever could, but still, if the church was willing to pay me, I wasn't going to say no.

I am not sure it was so much a case of being unwilling as it was that they couldn't afford to. Years before, when I had transitioned from child to youth leadership, I was standing in the office with the new volunteer for children's programs. We were organizing and planning when the pastor came into the room. He thanked us for everything that we were doing. He wanted us to know how valuable we were. Then he said, "I want you to know that you have been doing an incredible job, and when we can, we would really like to pay you." I looked at the children's director, and she had a huge smile. She said, "He's talking to you."

I had been told many times over the years by several different pastors that if the church could afford to pay me, they should, or would, depending on the pastor. It wasn't because I asked. I had never asked about collecting a paycheck, not until I sent Pastor Jason that message. Over the next week, Pastor Jason and I had several conversations, but we still hadn't talked about the message I had sent.

I finally got up the nerve to ask about it. I was sitting at a table in the back of the church, and Pastor Jason passed by on his way to the kitchen. "Pastor, did you get my message?" "Which message?" he asked. Oh great, now I was going to have to say it out loud. I could feel my heart racing. To this day, I don't understand why I was reacting so dramatically. "The one about getting paid for youth ministry," I replied. Not that he needed it, but I reassured him that a paycheque wasn't extremely important to me, but that youth ministry was and that I would still give 100% regardless of the answer. I am usually pretty good at setting my emotions aside. I hate crying in front of people, but there I was, having a mini emotional breakdown for reasons I didn't even understand. I legitimately, in my heart, did not care if I got paid. So why was this so intense? Perhaps it's because it was a defining moment. Maybe God was kickstarting something that I couldn't see. When I apologized for my display of emotions, Pastor said it was totally understandable, that it usually happens when people are very passionate about something. Pastor *had* seen my message. He said it was definitely something that we should look into. That sounded very familiar.

It was over a year later when I was sitting around a table with other church board members. The next topic of discussion was a slight increase in church income and whether or not we would like to hire someone to help out around the church. Wait a minute, *what*? Was this for real? The pastor went on to explain what the different possibilities could be, and where we could use the extra help. I was confused. I was also surprised, but not in a good way. I could feel my heart begin to pound in my chest.

I excused myself. I thought that a quick trip to the washroom might give me enough time to pull myself together. It didn't. The church had the resources to hire someone to help out but didn't have the resources to hire me? I could see years of promises being broken right before my eyes. I'm not going to sugarcoat it; I was upset, really upset. I had told myself that a paycheque didn't matter, but at that moment, I felt overlooked, like they didn't see the value in the work that I was doing, and that mattered! I was fighting back the tears that were welling up inside of me. Pastor Jason knew me well; we had worked together for years. As soon as we made eye contact, he knew that I wasn't OK.

Different board members made suggestions of what a new hire could do. I didn't want to say anything because I knew if I let even one word come out of my mouth, a flood of emotions was coming with it, but I couldn't keep what I was thinking to myself. "If you're going to hire someone to do something around the church, then you should hire them to be your youth leader." The room went silent. Finally, someone asked, "What do you mean?" My voice was shaky, and my eyes were full of tears. I wasn't being emotional; I was being real. What was happening around that table was hurtful. I said, "You're looking for something to pay someone to do while I'm working as the youth leader for free." I hated that I wasn't able to put my intense feelings aside and just talk about this, but I suppose that passion that Pastor Jason mentioned the last time we talked about it hadn't gone anywhere.

Pastor asked the board members to give us a minute. I was glad he did. We were friends, so it was a little less embarrassing to have an emotional meltdown with him and not with everyone on the board.

"Sarah," he said, "are you saying that if we bring someone else on staff that you are going to quit?"

I said softly, "I don't know." That's all I could say. "I don't know." I don't remember what else we discussed before the other board members returned, but I know I didn't say much. Pastor Jason probably used his coaching techniques to talk me down. He was pretty good at that. Not that I had ever needed it before. When it came to working with the teens, I was the one that helped others through a tough time. Although I remember having conversations with Pastor Jason where I would jokingly ask him if he was practicing his coaching techniques on me. This time it was no joke. I was going to need some time to clear my head, to figure out what I was really thinking.

Turns out I didn't need the time to figure it out. Pastor's explanation to the board members when they returned really summed it up. Pastor Jason had never promised me anything, but he knew that other pastors had. He told the board that for years the church had been dangling a carrot in front of me. I had never thought of it like that, but yes, that was the perfect way to de-

scribe it.

One of the board members said the slight increase in the church's income wouldn't be enough to pay me what I was worth. That it would be an insult to offer what they could afford. Did that even make sense? They couldn't pay me what they thought I should be paid, so they decided not to pay me at all?

We tabled the conversation for another time. Regardless of what I said to the board, I never wanted to give up youth ministry. I always thought that unless God said otherwise, I would give youth ministry everything I had until Levi, my youngest, graduated from high school. I didn't want to quit. It was a moment of weakness or perhaps a moment of strength; either way, it had started a conversation.

Over the next several months, Pastor Jason and I had very open and candid discussions about it. We talked about how it would be good if I could contribute to my family financially. The kids didn't have an issue with the amount of time I spent at the church or with other teens, but it would be nice if that meant I could help them save for college. Pastor and I joked about a T-shirt Tim had found that said, "Yet another Father's Day T-shirt that I paid for with my own money." It really was funny because it was true. I hadn't run my photography business for years, so Tim paid for everything, even his own Father's Day gifts. After church one Sunday, the same lady who had stood up in the annual meeting and asked if the church was willing to pay me, told me that I was doing a good job and that my reward was in Heaven. I smiled and said, "That's true, but my bills are on Earth."

I didn't know anything about it then, but behind the scenes,

Pastor Jason was making things happen. I had sporadic office hours working at the church. I went in and got things done whenever I could. This included 7:30 to 9:30 on Tuesday evenings. Braxton and Levi had basketball practice, so while they were in town, I would spend the evening catching up on youth programming. The church was empty on Tuesday evenings, and although I liked midday chats with the pastor, the ladies in the kitchen, the maintenance guys, and anyone else who happened to come through, I definitely got more accomplished when I was alone.

This Tuesday evening, I was not alone. I drove into the parking lot and parked beside a row of vehicles. I recognized them. They belong to Pastor Jason and the board members. Was I missing something? Was I supposed to be there? It must be important if the board is there, but I'm on the board, so it can't be a board meeting. I walked past the room where they were meeting on my way to the office. I heard my name. They weren't talking to me, so they must have been talking about me. I was either getting hired, or I was getting fired. I walked into the office and was tempted to leave the door open so that I might be able to hear what the meeting was about, but I closed the door behind me and told myself that it was really none of my business.

A few days later, I received an email. It was sent to my email address, but it clearly wasn't for me. It was addressed to the other members of the board, and the subject line read something like this: *Hiring Sarah Coombs as Youth Director.* I started to read the email, but it really wasn't for me, and I knew it. After the first few sentences, I felt guilty. I could tell that it had been sent to me by mistake, so I stopped reading, closed my laptop, and pretended I hadn't seen it.

When the Pastor called me into his office later that week, I knew what it was about, and he knew that I knew what it was about. He said, "I wanted to surprise you," as he pulled a large brown envelope from his desk drawer. "But I'm pretty sure you saw the email." I nodded. He handed me the envelope and said, "We would like to hire you as our Youth Director."

Funny, you would think that this is when I would be overcome with emotion. Maybe shed some tears, jump up on my chair, and do a happy dance. I would get to do what I love and get paid for it! I was happy, for sure, but I had a question. He asked me if I was interested, and I said, "Yes, but I need to know what your expectations would be." I loved my students, I loved youth ministry; it was my passion, my calling, and that is why for years, I had been treating it like it was a full-time job. If the board was to bring me on staff, would they be expecting more? Pastor assured me that my job description wouldn't include anything extra except perhaps speaking a little more often in the Sunday service. That was OK. I had already been filling in when Pastor was away, so I knew that that was something I could handle.

The day I was officially hired with the board, one of the members was on his way out of the room. He looked over his shoulder and said, "I expect to see you double the amount of teens in our church. More bang for our buck." He laughed it off, but I sensed some seriousness in what he said. I looked over at the Pastor. He just shrugged his shoulders and, with a smile, said, "Just keep doing what you're doing."

Pastor had said that it would be a long process and there would be a lot of paperwork to fill out. Inside the large brown envelope he gave me was an application form. It wasn't a standard online version; it was in-depth with several personal questions. I had no problem filling it out. I think it was helpful that the job I was applying for was one I had already been doing for 15 years. The people I needed to impress had already seen what I was able to do.

For the most part, I took the application process very seriously, but when it came to the part that asked where I saw myself in five, ten, and fifteen years, I couldn't resist. I took a picture of myself and, using an aging photo program, I created three pictures. In the five-year picture, I looked the same; in the ten-year picture, I gave myself wrinkles, and in the fifteen-year picture, I kept my eyes and hair but superimposed a 90-year-old lady's face over mine. Man, it was not pretty. I used a paper clip and attached the passport-size photos to my application with a note that said this is where I see myself in fifteen years. Pastor kept the pictures; I saw them in his desk drawer. No doubt they were saved for a chance to embarrass me in the future.

Pastor Jason said when I took on the staff position that things would be different. He would no longer be just my pastor, but he would be my boss. I was good with that. I already considered him my boss. I would tell people that "God hired me and that Jesus was my boss," but I always considered the pastors I worked with to be the authority in my ministry. I'm unsure if Pastor Jason had noticed, but I had started calling him boss several months before I was hired. He would walk into the office, and I would greet him with, "Hey, boss, how's it going?"

One of the changes that went along with being hired as a

staff member was a strong recommendation that I work on my pastor credentials, so I did. I was officially Pastor Sarah, which came in handy when Pastor Jason and his family moved away. The church hired me as a temporary lead pastor until they found another pastor to lead our church. You can say it was convenient or more likely a part of God's plan all along.

It had been almost two years since I sat at my laptop and debated whether or not to push the send button. I'm glad I did. I was pursuing the passion for young people that God had placed in my heart so many years before. He had blessed me with the opportunity to work in youth ministry, and now He was blessing me with a paycheck as well.

And we know that in all things, God works for the good of those who love him, who have been called according to his purpose.

Romans 8:28

Chapter 10

Claiming My Title

"I needed to knock that little devil off my shoulder and start answering those questions with the answers that had been the truth all along. I was good enough. I was strong enough."

~Sarah Jane

I had a trusted friend once tell me that my level of confidence could probably be intimidating to some people. I thought, "My, *what*?" We were texting back and forth, and I typed L.O.L. But I did more than just type it. I was legitimately laughing out loud. I wasn't confident at all. I was competent, that was for sure. If I was given a job to do, I would do it, and I would do it well, but confident, not so much. No matter how good I was at my job, the question was always there. Am I good enough? I texted them back and said, "I'm laughing because that confidence is totally fake." I may have looked confident on the outside but was quiet and timid and a little insecure on the inside. That was the day I diagnosed myself with fake confidence syndrome.

Apparently, fake confidence was something I had mastered. There was a time I accidentally tricked a personality test. A group of ladies from the church were starting a series. It was a Bible study about discovering your strengths. One of the first things we did was a personality test. It was just a fun quiz. I had done the in-depth personality tests before, but this was definitely a simplified version. The result would let you know what animal you were like, a quiet mouse, a charging bull, or maybe something in between. I don't remember all the questions, but I remember that it was nothing deep or serious.

One of the questions was, "What is your favorite color?" My favorite color changes with time and depends on the circumstances. I would love a pair of lime green high-top shoes, but I wouldn't paint my house that color. I'm not a fan of the color red, but when the tamarack trees around my house turn in the fall, I love that they turn red. At the time of the personality quiz, I was wearing a bright orange leather fall jacket. I loved that jacket. I liked the color orange, so at that moment, orange was my favorite color.

When we added the scores from our answer sheet, my score lined up with a roaring lion. My personality, according to the quiz, was that of a roaring lion. Really? I don't know that there had ever been a time when I felt like a roaring lion. The description that went with that was something along the lines of bold and confident. I had a theory that saying my favorite color was orange possibly put me in the bold category. I liked the idea of being a roaring lion, but it didn't line up with the timid kitten that was inside of me. There were two of us in the group whose results were the same. When I saw the other lion in the hallway on my way out of the building, she stopped me to tell me how much she really liked my bright orange jacket. I guess that backed up my theory.

I had never been an upfront, look-at-me kind of person. Sitting at the back of the class and trying not to get noticed was more my thing. Actually, not the back of the class. Those were the seats saved for the stereotypical rebels. I was more of a sit-in-the-middle-of-the-room kind of person, right behind the class clown and the smarty-pants, but never at the front.

In grade school, our class had to write and present speeches. We could do them on any topic that we wanted. I had read a book from the church library about Colonel Sanders, the Kentucky Fried Chicken guy. His life story was interesting and funny. I wrote my speech about him. It was a good speech. It kept everyone's attention and made my class laugh. I placed fourth in the classroom competition, so I got to—or should I say had to—present my speech on the stage in front of the whole school. I was nervous. I wanted everyone to hear the cool story about Colonel Sanders, but I really, really didn't want to stand up on the stage and try to speak in front of a large group of people.

I'd love to say that I overcame my insecurities, and the speech was a hit. But I didn't, and it wasn't. It was terrible. I stumbled over my words, messed up my cue cards, and totally forgot to include the funny stuff about Kentucky Fried Chicken. I wasn't happy that I messed up in front of everyone, but I was happy that I would not be picked to say it again at the next level of the competition. I didn't have the confidence for public speaking. I was perfectly happy letting someone else do the talking. I think that's how I got labeled a good listener.

I was sitting behind a boy in class one day when the teacher asked everyone to write down two things that they liked about the person sitting behind them. Then the teacher read out the compliments to the class. The teacher said, "Sarah, the person in front of you likes the way you tie your shoes, and he thinks that you are a good listener." The way I tie my shoes? Yep, that made sense. I used to weave my laces back and forth, up and down, and make a cool pattern on the top of my shoes. That compliment made sense, but a good listener? That wasn't the first time that someone had said that I was a good listener. Honestly, I just thought that was what a person would say if they couldn't think of anything nice to say about you. They could just say you were a good listener. I didn't realize that being a good listener was actually a thing. I just enjoyed listening more than I enjoyed speaking.

It's ironic how as a pastor in youth ministry, it became my job to speak; speak to teens, speak to their parents, speak in front of small groups, and speak in front of large groups. I had literally become a public speaker.

The fact that I was quiet and shy and spent more time listening than talking didn't stop God from calling me into youth ministry. It didn't seem to matter that a typical youth pastor was a little louder and, at times, a whole lot crazier than me. I remember being at a northern youth event with nearly 100 students and a dozen youth leaders. The worship band was playing, and everyone was super hyped. I watched as youth leaders made their way to the front. They started jumping up and down and waving their arms in the air. Insecurity, a lack of confidence, or perhaps a little devil on my shoulder began to play with my mind, telling me, "That is what a real youth pastor should look like." But that wasn't me. It wasn't my personality. I didn't want to be upfront, and

I didn't want to be jumping up and down. I'd given birth to four children, so if I had jumped up and down that dramatically, I probably would have peed my pants. I knew that there were times in youth ministry when I was going to have to get out of my comfort zone, speak a little louder, and muster up some fake confidence, but this was not one of those times. It made no difference to my students if I was dancing at the front or giving them a high-five when they returned to their seats, yet it still made me question myself. I had a passion, a deep desire to work with students, but was I a real youth pastor?

My friend, a doctor, was telling me about something called impostor syndrome. Apparently, a lot of people in the medical field struggle with this. She said that impostor syndrome can make a person doubt themselves or suffer from a lack of confidence regardless of their years of education or experience. She said imposter syndrome can leave people asking themselves what they are doing there and telling themselves that they don't belong, that they are a fraud. She had no idea how much I could relate to this. It didn't matter that I had my Biblical certificate or had been doing child or youth ministry since high school. There were still times when I asked myself, "Am I really good enough? Am I really spiritually strong enough?" That is when I decided that it was time to claim my title. I was a real youth pastor, and I needed to knock that little devil off my shoulder and start answering those questions with the answers that had been the truth all along. I *was* good enough. I *was* strong enough.

The Bible says that I can do all things when I do it through the strength that God has given me. This Bible verse, along with my experience in ministry, taught me that all I really needed to do was trust God. He called me into it, and He gave me everything I needed. When I needed to be strong, He made me strong. When I had to be creative, He flooded my mind with ideas. When it was time to make a tough decision, He gave me wisdom. When I needed to stop being quiet and timid, get up, and speak to a large group of people, God would give me the confidence to do it.

Speaking to my local teens was never really a struggle for me; they were my comfort zone, but asking me to get up in front of a group of anyone else, well, that was a different story.

I liked writing messages, and I looked forward to sharing them. The truth is, I wanted to speak; I really did. I'd even get excited about it, regardless of how large the group would be. But that excitement only lasted until the night before. That's when I asked myself, "Why did I agree to this? What was I thinking?" I would be torn between wanting to do this and do it well and being so nervous that my hands were shaking and butterflies were doing loops in my stomach. This is how I felt while I waited for my turn to go on stage.

But that's when God would show up. He would give me everything I needed to do what he had called me to do. It would never fail that during the last worship song before I went up on stage, my hands would stop shaking, the butterflies in my stomach would fly away, and peace would come over me. I would say an unexplainable peace, but I could explain it. It was God's way of saying, "Move over, Sarah; Holy Spirit coming through." Eventually, I began trusting that God would show up. I still had shaky hands and butterflies before a speaking engagement, but I knew that when the last worship song played that God would give me the confidence to do what he wanted me to do.

A friend and I used to go for coffee every couple of weeks. She was new in town, and her son had started going to our youth group. I say we went for coffee, but neither of us actually drank coffee. She would order a fancy tea with almond milk, oat milk, or whatever gave her tea a healthy twist. On the other hand, I would order a white hot chocolate with a strawberry, orange, or caramel flavor shot. We would pick up our drinks and go for walks through the park, getting to know each other better. This friend was consistently excited about one thing or another, and she always had plenty to say. I was more on the quiet side. Every once in a while, she would stop talking and say, "You've hardly said anything; it's your turn. I want to know what you're thinking." It was true that I hadn't said much, partly because this friend talked a lot, but mostly because I liked listening to her stories. Her name was Julie. Julie had never heard me preach. Her son had been to plenty of our youth activities, and he had seen me in action, but Julie had only seen the side of me that was quiet and reserved.

During one of our larger youth events, I asked Julie if she would like to help out at the registration table. She registered the students, entered their names in a drawing, and showed them to their seats. Then she sat at the registration table, where she had a good view of what was happening on the platform. The final worship song played, and God did what he always did before I hit the stage. I got up and spoke a powerful and energized message. When I was finished speaking, Julie found me. In the vividly enthusiastic way that I had come to love, she said, "What was that? Who are you? Where did that come from? You were on fire up there. You're a rockstar!" I really did appreciate her compliments, but she was wrong. I wasn't a rockstar any more than I had been a roaring lion years before. But God was. He was the rockstar. He was the roaring lion. My strength and my boldness, and my ability to speak a powerful and energized message came from him. He gave me everything I needed. He always has.

I realized that the self-diagnosed fake confidence syndrome had never been fake confidence. In those moments, God gave me exactly what I needed to do what He was calling me to do.

I can do all this through him who gives me strength.

Philippians 4:13 (NIV)

Chapter 11

Righteous Right Hand

I heard a quiet whisper. "You don't hold up this youth group; I do."

~Sarah Jane

If you look really hard in the storage room in my basement, you'll find an old 80s-style school bag. In the bag, you will find 120 yo-yos of various sizes, shapes, and colours. My yo-yo collection used to be in a display case, proudly displayed on the walls of our apartments. As we moved from one town to another, the yo-yos eventually ended up in a bag, and the glass in the display case was broken. I started collecting yo-yos when I worked at camp as a teenager. Everyone had a thing. For one person, it was their crazy sunglasses; for another, their bright yellow Sun Zinc lips, and someone else sported fancy shoelaces. For me, it was my yo-yo. I found my first yo-yo on the ground after the campers left one Saturday. My second yo-yo came from the lost and found. For a while, I was a master of the yo-yo. I could rock the cradle, walk the dog, go around the world and back again. My only yo-yo trick today would be trying not to hit myself in the head when the yo-yo bounces back up the string.

Tim and I both had nicknames that summer. That's where

he got the nickname Zip. As the sports director, he ruled the high ropes course, especially the 100-foot zip line. Originally, he was The Zipper, but it was shortened to Zipper by the other camp staff. Today, I just call him Zip. My nickname was Yo-Yo, and it died at the end of the summer. That summer, I was known for saying two things. Actually, singing one of them and saying the other. To the tune of *Row Row Row Your Boat*, I would sing, "Yo yo yo your yo-yo up and down the string, merrily, merrily, merrily, merrily, life is a wonderful thing." I was working with children at the time, so I guess it's OK that this sounds extremely childish to me now. My other saying was, "Life is like a yo-yo; sometimes you're up, sometimes you're down." At the beginning of my youth ministry, this is exactly how I felt. One Friday night, I would walk away on top of the world, a spiritual high. The students would have invited friends, and it seemed like everyone understood the message. Another time, I would walk away shaking my head and asking myself, "Why do I even bother?"

I did a series with my junior youth program about dealing with your emotions. I called it *Dealing with Your Emojis* because that sounded like a whole lot more fun. The first lesson dealt with two emojis, the happy face and the sad face. The idea was that God doesn't want us to be riding on an emotional roller coaster or to be up and down like an emoji yo-yo. He wants us to experience the joy of the Lord, even when things aren't going so great.

Working with youth can be exciting; it's fun. Teenagers are the most creative and witty people on our planet. The teens I work with say and do the weirdest things. They dance like no one's watching in a room full of people. They make me laugh even when I'm trying to be serious. They are smart. They are brave. They are stronger than they even know. But these same teenagers wake up every day to face some really dark realities. Life isn't always easy; sometimes it's hard, really hard, and teenagers experience that firsthand. I've worked with teenagers from broken homes, teens caught up in addiction, victims of abuse or neglect, and others who suffer from depression or anxiety. Their loads are heavy. There were very few times that I didn't feel the weight of their struggles. As the youth pastor, I felt spiritually responsible for our teens, and that's a heavy load to carry. At times, I could feel myself sinking under the weight of that responsibility.

When I pray for people, I have a habit of starting out my prayer by lifting them up to God. For example, if I was praying for someone named Sue, I would pray, "Dear God, I want to lift Sue up to you right now." If I was praying for someone named George, I might say, "God, I'm lifting George up to you." I guess it was my way of saying that I was giving them to Him for help.

One night I was praying for our youth group, not individuals, but the entire youth ministry as a whole. I just started out by saying, "Dear God, I am lifting up this youth group to you," and then I had a vision, one that completely changed the way I view youth ministry. In the vision, there was a giant hand, a strong hand with a firm grip. It was holding up a serving tray or a plate of some kind. On top of the tray was a group of teens. The tray hung over the side of the hand, and hanging off the tray was another person. They weren't actually hanging off the tray. They were underneath the edge of it with their hands lifted up as if they were holding up the tray full of students, but they weren't. Their feet were dangling in the air. A second hand came down, and, using the pointer finger and thumb, it picked up the person dangling under the tray and placed them on top with a group of teens.

I knew exactly what it meant. That was me. I was the person dangling underneath the tray, try-ing to hold it up. I heard a quiet whisper. "You don't hold up this youth group; I do." In the vision, God had picked me up and put me on the tray. He was carrying the weight. I couldn't lift this youth group up to him because he was already holding us in his hand. Whenever

Righteous Right Hand

I think about this, I remember what the Bible says in Isaiah 41:10 that God "will strengthen you and help you. He will uphold you with his righteous right hand." I had seen the righteous right hand of God in my vision. The image was powerful. I didn't need to carry the weight of youth minis-try on my shoulders when God was carrying it in his hand. I thought the illustration was too good not to share.

I'm a big fan of visuals in church, so I taped a 6 x 4 sheet of thick brown paper to the wall at the front of the room. I penciled in a drawing of a giant hand holding up a group of teens and a person dangling beneath them. As I spoke that Sunday morning, two girls from the youth group used ex-tra thick black markers and paint to trace out the drawing.

The audience could not see the pencil marks, but as the girls painted the lines, everyone could see the vision that I was sharing.

I've heard people say that God won't give you more than you can handle, or in the middle of an overwhelming challenge, they'll say, "You got this," but sometimes I didn't "have this." I couldn't handle things on my own, and I didn't have to. I was never really on my own. God wasn't only holding me up; he was holding up the entire youth ministry.

Someone once asked me, "How do you manage to do all this?" I don't know if they asked because of the children's program and youth activities I had been running or because I had four children wrapped around my legs. That wasn't the first time; I'd been asked that question many times throughout the years. Whenever someone asked me, I would be reminded of an old hymn we used to sing in church. It was written over 100 years ago. If you dusted off an old songbook, you'd probably find it in there. I didn't pay much attention to the lyrics when I sang them in church as a kid, but several years later, I listened to them over and over again. When I lived in Lindsay, there was a bookstore that sold cassettes. Yes, cassettes; it was a long time ago. Not many people still had cassette players, but we had one in the car. The bookstore had a clearance bin beside the cash register. That's where I found the cassette. It was old church songs put to some cool electro music. That got my attention.

The song was "He Giveth More Grace." It was about how when we're tapped out and have no strength left that God's strength is only beginning.

When we have exhausted our store of endurance,

When our strength has failed ere the day is half done,
When we reach the end of our hoarded resources
Our Father's full giving is only begun.

I decided that if anyone else asked me, "How do I do it?" I'd just say, "When we reach the end of our hoarded resources, our Father's full giving is only begun." They might have no clue what I was talking about, but it would be fun to say. There was some real truth in those lyrics. If I wasn't strong enough, it didn't matter because God was. I couldn't have done any of this on my own. It was his righteous right hand that was holding me up.

So do not fear, for I am with you; do not be dismayed, for I am your God. I will strengthen you and help you; I will uphold you with my righteous right hand.

Isaiah 41:10

Chapter 12

They Can Hear You

"Maybe you've asked yourself the same question: are my words powerful? The answer is yes! Someone is listening to you, and your words do have the power to make a difference."

~ Sarah Jane

"Your son doesn't pay attention in class," the teacher said. Not exactly how you want a parent-teacher interview to start off. "But he hears everything I say." Oh, ok, that sounded better. The teacher explained how my son Braxton always seems distracted in class. She often saw him staring out the window, drawing in his books, or playing with his shoelaces. She assumed he wasn't listening. He didn't keep eye contact with her and definitely was not hanging off every word she said. It was as if he was in his own world. She said, "I don't know how he does it; if I ask him what we're talking about, he always knows." She thought that he wasn't listening, but he was. He heard and remembered everything she said.

I am normally a pretty quiet person with not a whole lot to say, but when it comes to youth ministry and speaking with the teens, you couldn't get me to stop talking. I could spend hours preparing a powerful message, a lesson that packs a punch, or an inspirational speech. Yet I would often find myself asking, are they really, are the messages *really* powerful? Do the lessons *really* pack a punch? Was that speech *really* inspirational? Do the words that I speak make an impact? Does my ministry make a difference in the lives of the students that I work with? At the end of the day, do they hear me and remember anything I say? Maybe you've asked yourself the same question; are my words powerful? The answer is yes! Someone is listening to you, and your words do have the power to make a difference.

I didn't think that James was listening. James was a part of Rooted Youth Ministry for several years. He often wandered off for months at a time but always managed to find his way back. After camp each summer, the students were given the opportunity on a Sunday morning to take the mic. They were asked to share stories from their week away. When it was James' turn to share a story, he didn't talk about camp. He talked about Rooted Youth and how it had been like a family to him. He said that Sarah (that's me) had said something earlier in the summer that had a huge impact on his life. James was quite the character, and I had no idea what would come out of his mouth, but I was even more curious about what had come out of mine. What did I say to him?

My mind raced back over the last month to try and remember any deep, meaningful conversation I may have had with James. I couldn't remember any profound wisdom or sound advice I had given him. Now I was really curious. He spoke directly into the mic and said, "Sarah told me that she was proud of me," then he said, "No one has ever told me that before." Wow, I couldn't even remember telling James that I was proud of him, but it definitely was something I would have thought, and I'm glad I shared my thoughts with him. Clearly, he was listening. The Bible says that the tongue has the power of life or death. Our words can speak life or death into the people around us. Telling James that I was proud of him was not a big deal to me; I didn't even remember saying it. But those words spoke life into James's situation.

I was on the phone with a young woman the other day. She was a part of our youth program growing up and still gives me a call when she's going through hard times. This young lady shared with me her heartache and her trouble. Then she told me that when she's really going through a difficult time, she thinks of this poem. She had memorized the poem and recited it over the phone for me.

From a child to a woman

All fast forward no rewind

See your moment in the future

Leave the hurt and scars behind

Standing in the mirror

See the pain of yesterday

Letting go and stepping forward

Let forgiveness lead the way

I said, "I like it; that's a pretty good poem." She started to laugh just a little. I said, "What? It's got a powerful message. Why are you laughing? Did you write it?" She said, "No, you did."

She was right. I had written that poem for her many years

before. I had forgotten about it, but she had not and had memorized every word. It wasn't a spoken word; it was a written word, but the results were the same. If she had never told me about it, I would not have known that those words were an inspiration for her so many years later.

Sometimes we need to be reminded that someone is listening and that our words make a difference.

I have a secret drawer under my bed. The drawer itself is not a secret. It's my T-shirt drawer, no mystery there, but I've never told anyone what's tucked away behind the T-shirts. There is a stack of lighters that used to belong to teens that I worked with. They weren't confiscated; I was asked to take them. Over time, various youths have given them to me. They wanted to make a change, and part of that change meant they no longer needed a lighter in their pocket. There are two knives at the back of the drawer as well. They are both from the same student. I was asked to hold on to these knives by a student who was overcoming her struggle with self-harm. Next to the knives is a stack of letters, a collection of thank you notes from some of the teenagers that were in the youth program. It's been a really long time since one of the teens passed me a handwritten thank-you note. My thank yous now come in the form of a text, an Instagram message, or a funny "couldn't do it without you" GIF or meme. I don't make it a habit of saving texts or memes, but I did save those letters. If I ever ask myself if what I'm doing makes a difference, if anyone is listening, I just have to read some of the words on the pages of those letters.

"You make me think that my life isn't all bad and that there is more for me to live for in the future, so all I want to say is

*thank you."~*13-year-old girl

"You are the first person, and I mean very first person who makes me feel good about myself." ~14-year-old girl

"Thank you for everything you've done for me. For every-thing you've helped me with or helped me through. You've impacted my life tremendously. If I didn't have you to talk to I don't know where my life would be right now. I know I was stubborn at first, not wanting help but you fought through and I couldn't thank you more for that." ~15-year-old girl

"...I just really appreciated how you showed how much you cared and that you were always there for me if I needed it and I just really looked up to you." ~19-year-old boy

*"If it wasn't for you I wouldn't be alive right now."~*16-year-old girl

"Honestly I'll never be able to thank you enough for showing me that; Through God all things are possible." ~14-year-old girl

In many of these thank you letters, texts, or conversations, there seemed to be a recurring theme that I had somehow changed their lives. But the truth is, I didn't do that. I may have taught them things they needed to know. I may have encouraged them or challenged them. For some, I may have held them while they cried, but I didn't change their lives. God did that! Nothing I have ever said or will ever say will be as powerful as the word of God. God's word, His prom-ises, His lessons, His truths, His messages, that's where the powerful words really are. When I say God's words, I'm talking about solid biblical truth. That's what changes lives!

I've learned a lot about farming in the past couple of years. Tim and my son Ben spent hours in the field planting crops. Their hard work was rewarding when they saw the crop start to grow, when perfect rows of green leaves started coming through the dirty soil, and even more rewarding when they started bringing in the harvest at the end of the season.

In youth ministry, I was planting seeds in the lives of the students that I worked with. When those seeds started growing, and a student's life started to change, I was encouraged and motivated to keep planting more seeds. In reality, that's all that I could do, plant seeds. The growing and the changing were in God's hands.

There is a lesson in the Bible. It's found in 1 Corinthians 3:6,7 (NIV). A group of people were arguing over who they should follow. Should they follow Paul, or should they follow Apollos? Paul steps in and says that it isn't about either of them. He tells the people to follow God. He says, "I planted the seed, Apollos watered it, but God has been making it grow. So neither the one who plants nor the one who waters is anything, but only God, who makes things grow."

It's encouraging to know that telling James that I was proud of him impacted his life or that a poem I wrote for a student many years ago still brings her comfort today. Those thank-you letters tucked away in the back of my T-shirt drawer remind me that someone is listening. When I talk about God's love, teach about Jesus, speak on forgiveness, and preach the word of God, things change because God begins to work in the lives of the students who are listening. And yes, they *are* listening, and my words *do* make a difference.

So neither the one who plants nor the one who waters is any-thing, but only God, who makes things grow.

1 Corinthians 3:7

Chapter 13

It's Not About You

"When you have no idea what you want to do next in your life, then you are in the perfect place for God to call you into something that you may never have thought of on your own. I was in that place."

~Sarah Jane

We were sitting at a round table in the Life Centre, an addition to the church built several years earlier. This is where the new pastor and I held our staff meetings every Tuesday morning. We would discuss the week gone by, and I would fill him in on the schedule for upcoming youth events. That Tuesday morning, I told the pastor about a plan that had been in the works for a long time.

It had been almost 16 years since I started the youth program in Kapuskasing. I loved students, cared about them, and prayed for them for years. I had prepared countless messages, lessons, and Bible series. I had planned youth events, Friday night activities, evening drop-ins, weekend adventures, mission trips, and so much more. Almost 16 years of doing what I truly loved to do. But it was time to let it go.

The pastor seemed surprised to hear that I would be leaving the ministry. It was never meant to be a surprise. It was no secret that Levi's final year of high school would be my final year working with the students. My passion for youth ministry hadn't faded, and neither had my love for the teens. My deep desire to see their lives impacted through youth ministry had not changed. It was my plans that had changed.

Tim was still working for Sunwing in Toronto. He was in the sky more than on the ground, traveling from one vacation destination to another. If someone else was running the youth program, I could travel with him and take in a few vacation destinations myself.

Victoria and her husband Kyle were living in Ottawa. Kyle was away for work. Victoria had her hands full with two very rambunctious boys and baby number three on the way. If I handed the youth ministry over to someone else, I could use Tim's discount flights to go and visit Victoria and the boys. Our family had always been involved in ministry, so I never felt torn between raising a family and giving a hundred percent to the teens I worked with. But Victoria had moved nine hours away, and I was beginning to feel like I was missing out on something special. I wanted to spend more time with her and the boys. When Victoria was feeling overwhelmed, I didn't want to just tell her over the phone that things would get better. I wanted to be there, in person, helping out and making things easier for her.

I like planning ahead. That's the kind of person I am. I plan things in advance and make to-do lists. That's how I get things done. I put them on a list, and then I make them happen. I like to-do lists so much that if I've done something that's not on my list, I will add it just so I can cross it off. Yes, I realize I probably need therapy for my to-do list addiction, but it works for me. Stepping out of youth ministry when Levi stepped out of high school was on my mental to-do list. I let the Pastor know that in a year and a half, I would be transitioning out of my position as youth pastor.

I had a plan. Braxton would be away at university, Levi would be off to college, and Ben would be home or away, depending on his work and school schedule. I was sure Benjamin would miss the home-cooked meals and piles of washed and folded laundry on his bed when he came home from work, but he was an adult and didn't need me to take care of him. When my time in youth ministry was over, I was going to travel. Hit the skies with my favorite pilot and stop in for some quality time with Victoria and her boys.

What happened next was a clear case of expectations vs reality. My expectation was that this plan was really going to happen. The reality was very different. Braxton came home after his first year at university. He needed some time to figure out what he wanted to do next. Levi decided to do a victory lap and get in one more year of high school basketball before he went to college. The Covid pandemic took my husband from full-time pilot to full-time farmer in a matter of months. He had lost his job at Sunwing. No more vacation destinations and no more cheap flights to see Victoria. This was the reality. The house wasn't empty, it was full, and the only traveling that Tim was doing was back and forth across the field in a tractor.

At that moment, my life reminded me of a picture I had seen. The picture I saw was the Choluteca Bridge in Honduras, Central America when it was scheduled to open. The bridge was built to withstand hurricane winds and flash floods.

There had been a massive flood. The bridge was standing strong, but the flood had washed away the road on both ends of the bridge and diverted the river. The water was no longer flowing under the bridge. I could relate to this. I had been making solid plans based on the way things were. I hadn't expected that things would change so dramatically.

It was a while before the pastor and I had another discussion about my transition out of ministry. We were back at that round table in the Life Center. We discussed the previous week and upcoming events, and then he said softly, "I hate to bring this up, but we have to talk about you leaving." I could tell that he was trying to be sensitive. I had never said anything, but I'm sure he could tell that this time of transition wouldn't be easy for me. He was right. I got a little choked up every time I thought about it. I reassured him that it was OK to talk about me leaving. He didn't have to tiptoe around it. It was a fact; I was leaving youth ministry, and we needed to figure things out. I told him I would get emotional and might even cry, but it didn't matter; we still needed to talk about it. We needed to start looking for a new youth pastor for our teens.

Several months passed, and people started asking questions. One of the hardest questions to answer was, "Why are you giving up youth ministry?." If someone had asked me that a year before, I could've told them all about the wonderful plans I had for the next stage of my life. But now, not only was that question hard, but it broke my heart a little more every time someone asked. I didn't have an answer. I started asking myself the same question, "Why *am* I giving up youth ministry?" I loved my students and loved spending time with them, planning, organizing, and teaching about Jesus.

If I wasn't going to be traveling and I was going to be home, then why was I giving it up? That was a really good question.

Tim would joke about how I would have plenty of time to help him on the farm. I no longer had a plan for after youth ministry, but if I did, that wasn't it. A verse in the Bible teaches that God has plans for us and that those plans are good. It's found in Jeremiah 29:11. I had to believe God had a plan because *I* certainly did not.

I was driving into town one day when I heard a question asked on the radio. It was one of those morning call-in shows. The question was, "What is your dream job?" They asked, "If you could do any job, any job at all, what would you choose to do?" I was too wrapped up in my own thoughts to hear what anyone's answers were. I was taken back to the 'jump off the page' moment in the high school library and Miss White's English assignment about what we wanted to do with our lives. I had discovered what the grown-up version of a camp counselor was. It was a youth pastor, and that's what I was. I became painfully aware that in just a few months, I would be giving up my dream job.

We were going through the process of selecting a new youth leader. The pastor was exploring options. He was looking at Bible college graduates and youth pastors who were on job hunts. We considered the possibility that God would raise up someone from within the church. One person's name kept coming to my mind. I didn't even know if they were interested, but I could see what a good fit they might be. His name was Shawn, and he was already helping with our junior high program. I asked him if he would be interested in helping with the senior highs as well, and he started coming out to all of our events. He was good with the students, and they really seemed to like him. I could see he was serious about ministry and his relationship with God.

I thought Shawn might do a good job in youth ministry, but I tried not to think about it too much. I was really struggling with the idea of leaving youth work. I was OK during youth activities and hanging out with the teens. Maybe because I was too busy doing youth ministry to think about missing it. Sunday mornings were a different story. Every Sunday got harder and harder. I would stand with the teens singing praise and worship songs and fighting back the tears every week. I just kept asking myself if I was making a mistake. Was this God's plan for me, or was I on my own in this? Was I following where God was leading me, or was I only leaving youth ministry because it was on my mental to-do list from years ago? And if I was following God, then why was it so hard? I had a whirlwind of thoughts spinning in my head. I felt guilty for abandoning the youth, selfish for making my own plans, and thankful for the opportunity to work with so many amazing teenagers, but heartbroken over saying goodbye.

I stood with my hands out to God; I wasn't holding back the tears anymore. I was crying. My heart was aching. I'm just going to call it like it was. I was full-out throwing myself a pity party, but the emotions were real. I hadn't even stepped away from youth ministry yet, but I was missing it already. I stood there, wiping away the tears as I prayed. That's when I heard God speak. Throughout this entire process, I felt like God was distant. I didn't know if I was doing the right thing. But there it was. The unmistakable voice of God saying, "It's not about you." I turned my head slightly to the right, and Shawn was in the row in front of me. His arms were raised in the air as he worshiped God. It wasn't about me. It was about him.

That was a defining moment. That was the moment I stopped feeling sorry for myself. I stopped questioning if I had made the right choice. It was at that moment that I stopped feeling guilty and selfish at the same time. It wasn't about me. It never had been about me. It wasn't my youth ministry. It was God's, and it was time for someone else to lead it. Shawn had not been hired as our next youth leader, but I knew he would be.

I'd like to say that the pain of leaving youth ministry went away that day, but it didn't. Sundays were still hard. But I knew how to calm the mini-twister of emotions spinning in my head. I would look over at Shawn and remind myself that it wasn't about me.

After Shawn was hired, we started a somewhat quick transition. I wanted to talk to the students before it was announced in church. Most of our older students had known for a long time that this would be my last year. Some of them had asked me to stay one more year until they graduated, but I assured them that I wasn't going anywhere. I would still be in church on Sundays, and they could text me any time. They would be spending their Friday nights with Shawn, but if they really needed me, they knew where to find me.

The Friday before we announced in church, I met with the teens. The group was a bit larger that night. Everyone was excited to hear who the next youth leader would be. Earlier in the week, I had thought about giving Shawn something special. I thought it would be a good idea to have a "passing the torch" kind of moment when we announced that he would be taking over. I had decided that as hard as this was going to be, I needed to put a smile on my face. If I was excited about the transition, then the students would follow my lead, and they would also be excited about it.

I wished we had a new Rooted hoodie that I could wrap up and give to Shawn, but the hoodies were sold out as soon as we got them. I stood in front of my closet holding my own Rooted hoodie in my hands. Part of me wanted to give it to Shawn, but I couldn't. I couldn't let it go. I knew it was selfish, but I loved my Rooted hoodie. I was emotionally attached to it. I put the hoodie back in my closet and opened the T-shirt drawer under my bed. I pulled out my Rooted T-shirt. The T-shirt was older but still had precious memories that the new hoodie did not. I thought if I was symbolically passing the torch, this shirt would be perfect. It had been through years of youth ministry with me. I wrapped up the T-shirt and included a note.

That Friday night, I enthusiastically introduced Shawn as the next youth leader. I was determined to keep the atmosphere energized. I had not planned on crying. This was his moment, not mine, and I didn't want to be emotional about it. I put a smile on my face as I told the group that I would no longer be leading Rooted youth ministry. I'm not sure that the smile on my face could hide how hard it was to say those words. I looked into the faces of some of the older students sitting closer to the back. They had been on this journey with me for years. They weren't smiling back. There was a silent conversation taking place between us. They were saying, "If you don't cry, then I won't cry," and I was saying, "It's a deal."

I did a big build-up to announcing Shawn as the next youth leader. I might have even asked for a drumroll. Shawn made his way to the front. I hadn't expected Shawn to be emotional, but I could see it in his eyes. This wasn't just a big moment for me; it was a big moment for him as well. God was calling him into youth ministry just as He had called me many years before. I handed him the wrapped gift. He took the lid off the box and pulled out the Rooted T-shirt. Shawn held the note in his hands. I asked him if I could read it for the group. If I was trying not to cry, reading this note out loud was definitely a mistake. The note read:

Shawn:

This is for you. It's not new. It's old, probably 10 years now. It's mine, but now it's yours. It has bleach marks and stains but I see them as memories. Memories of spilled community dinners and kitchen clean ups, memories of ice cream cones on mission trips that melted too fast, memories of sandy beach days and backyard campfire smoke. This shirt has hugged a hundred people and had tears dropped on its arm sleeves as young people prayed together. It's your turn to wear the shirt. I hope and pray that you also have a chance to make lasting memories in this shirt. That when you wear it you will be blessed as much as I have been.

~Pastor Sarah

When I finished reading the note, Shawn and I both had tears in our eyes. That moment was a dealbreaker with the older students in the back, and they were wiping away their tears as well. As hard as it was to be passing on the youth ministry, I really was happy for him. I was excited to see how God would use Shawn as he worked with the teenagers.

Saying goodbye to the Rooted Youth program had been an emotional roller coaster, but the junior high program was very different. I hadn't planned to make a big deal out of the transition. I would lead the junior high students at the afterschool program until school was out at the end of June, and Shawn would kick it off again in September.

I didn't have the same connection with the junior highs as with the older teens. When the schools closed during Covid, I switched to online programming. We did some really cool stuff, and the students were engaged, but it wasn't a good way to build relationships. When we reopened the afterschool program, the students I had known for years had already moved into Rooted. Shawn has started volunteering at the afterschool program, so as new junior highs came in, Shawn was as much of a leader to them as I was.

I had announced on Friday night that I would be leaving youth ministry, and the pastor had announced it that Sunday in church. The next week when the junior highs arrived for the afterschool program, they were surprised to see me. One student asked, "Why are you here? I thought Shawn was our leader now." I suppose that could have hurt my feelings, but it didn't, not at all. I had to laugh. I could see that this would be an easy transition for the junior high kids.

June 26th was my final Sunday as the youth pastor at our church in Kapuskasing. They called it my retirement. That was weird for me. I was too young to retire. I figured that when you have been hired by God, and Jesus is your boss, you never really get to retire. As long as you have breath in your lungs, He will have a job for you. But this was my last day working for the church, so "retirement" was the word. Everyone congratulated me on my retirement. It felt extremely awkward. I quit my job, and yet everyone was congratulating me. I knew it was coming from a place of love, and I appreciated their kindness.

The following Sunday was the first youth activity that I was not involved in. I sat in my jeep across the street from the church parking lot and watched as the students loaded into Shawn's big white 12-passenger van. The van was a little beat up, but it was ideal for taking trips with the youth. My boys would make fun of it and call it the kidnapper van.

Youth programming was on Sunday afternoons for the summer months and the students were headed out on a hike to the falls. I had done that hike with them before. We walked the long trail through the bush. It was spring, and the trail was full of muddy puddles. Some of the puddles were so large that they covered the trail from one side to the other. We would hold onto the trees along the side of the trail, trying not to fall into the mud. The trail ended at the top of a hill with a rocky pathway to the rapids below. We had a picnic and devotions on the large stones along the river's shore. One of our older students had his lifeguard qualifications, so I let the students go into the water. They floated on logs down the slower part of the rapids and swam in the calmer water below the falls. Two guys found a large rock ledge in the middle of the river. They stood on it as we took pictures and joked about how they could walk on water. All these memories flooded back as I watched the students pack their things into the van. Once again, I felt myself fighting to hold back my tears, but they began to run down my cheeks as Tim and I drove away.

Each Sunday got a little easier. By the third Sunday, I had stopped tearing up when people would ask me if I missed youth ministry. After a while, I was able to joke about it. I told one of the guys from Rooted that I missed seeing him around. He said sarcastically, "Well, I guess you shouldn't have quit your job then." He was one of the students who had asked me to keep doing youth for one more year. He may have actually meant what he said, but he said it with a smile on his face. I just nodded my head and said, "That's fair."

It had been 29 years since I had felt God calling me to work with teenagers as I sat at the table in the high school library. He led me on an amazing journey through youth ministry. I felt His presence, heard His voice, and saw Him come alive in the lives of the teenagers I worked with. I had learned to trust Him as He gave me the strength to do what He had called me to do. I didn't know what was next. For the first time in a very long time, I didn't have a plan. I needed to trust that God did. Sometimes my students would struggle with life plans, panicking if they were almost finished high school and hadn't decided on their future. I told them, "When you have no idea what you want to do next in your life, then you are in the perfect place for God to call you into something that you may never have thought of on your own." I was in that place. The perfect place for God to put another "jump off the page" word in my life.

> *"For I know the plans I have for you," declares the Lord, "plans to prosper you and not to harm you, plans to give you hope and a future."*
>
> *Jeremiah 29:11 NIV*

www.ingramcontent.com/pod-product-compliance
Lightning Source LLC
Chambersburg PA
CBHW051319120626
46547CB00015B/2304